# Advanced SCAT Practice Tests

## Three Full-Length Verbal and Quantitative Mock Tests with Detailed Answer Explanations

Anthem Press
An imprint of Wimbledon Publishing Company
*www.anthempress.com*

This edition first published in UK and USA 2021
by ANTHEM PRESS
75–76 Blackfriars Road, London SE1 8HA, UK
or PO Box 9779, London SW19 7ZG, UK
and
244 Madison Ave #116, New York, NY 10016, USA

© Accel Learning LLC www.accellearning.com 2021

All rights reserved. Without limiting the rights under copyright reserved above, no part of this publication may be reproduced, stored or introduced into a retrieval system, or transmitted, in any form or by any means (electronic, mechanical, photocopying, recording or otherwise), without the prior written permission of both the copyright owner and the above publisher of this book.

British Library Cataloguing-in-Publication Data

A catalogue record for this book is available from the British Library.

Library of Congress Cataloging-in-Publication Data

A catalog record for this book has been requested.

ISBN-13: 978-1-83998-171-5 (Pbk)
ISBN-10: 1-83998-171-7 (Pbk)

This title is also available as an e-book.

# Contents

Introduction .................................................................................................. iv

**Practice Test 1** ........................................................................................... 1
   Verbal Practice Test ............................................................................... 2
   Quantitative Practice Test ..................................................................... 15
   Answer Key .......................................................................................... 29
   Answer Key with Explanations ............................................................. 30

**Practice Test 2** ......................................................................................... 41
   Verbal Practice Test ............................................................................. 42
   Quantitative Practice Test ..................................................................... 55
   Answer Key .......................................................................................... 69
   Answer Key with Explanations ............................................................. 70

**Practice Test 3** ......................................................................................... 81
   Verbal Practice Test ............................................................................. 82
   Quantitative Practice Test ..................................................................... 95
   Answer Key ........................................................................................ 109
   Answer Key with Explanations ........................................................... 110

# Introduction

The School and College Ability Test (SCAT) is a multiple-choice, standardized test administered by the Johns Hopkins Center for Talented Youth (CTY), a gifted education program for school-age children in the second to twelfth grades. It is an above-grade level test that assesses math and verbal reasoning abilities among gifted children and assesses students at a higher grade level than the one they are in at the time the test is administered.

Check here for more information about the CTY program: https://cty.jhu.edu/

There are three levels of SCAT:

1. Elementary Level SCAT – Students in grades 2–3 take the Elementary SCAT designed for students in grades 4–5.
2. Intermediate Level SCAT – Students in grades 4–5 take the Intermediate SCAT designed for students in grades 6–8.
3. Advanced Level SCAT - Students in grades 6 and above take the Advanced SCAT designed for students in grades 9–12.

The two sections for testing math and verbal reasoning are each 22-minutes long separated by a 10-minutes break. There are 55 multiple-choice questions per section, 5 of which are experimental.

The verbal section assesses the student's understanding of word definitions and consists of verbal reasoning analogy questions. In each question, students are presented with a pair of words that are related to each other in some way. They are then to select from the answer options a pair of words that shares the same relation.

The quantitative section assesses how well the student is able to work with numbers and consists of multiple-choice mathematical comparisons. Each question displays two quantities, of which the student needs to choose the one with the greater value.

Students are required to register with CTY to obtain an eligibility number before they can register to test at a Prometric test center. After receiving the eligibility number, students can book their SCAT test at the nearest Prometric test center by logging into their MyCTY account online here: https://cty.jhu.edu/talent/eligibility/index.html

Results of above-grade level assessments may confer the following eligibility levels:

- Advanced CTY Level: test scores that reflect ability approximately four grade levels above the current enrolled grade.
- CTY Level: test scores that reflect ability approximately two grade levels above the current enrolled grade.

Students may take the SCAT two times during any single academic year.

Students can view their results after taking the test on the John Hopkins MyCTY page here: https://mycty.jhu.edu/mycty2/login.cfm.

SCAT Scaled Scores are based on the number of questions the student answers correctly out of the 50 scored questions in each section. They range from 401 to 514 depending on the level the student takes as shown below:

- Elementary Level
  - Verbal Range = 401-471
  - Quantitative Range = 412-475
- Intermediate Level
  - Verbal Range = 405-482
  - Quantitative Range = 419-506
- Advanced Level
  - Verbal Range = 410-494
  - Quantitative Range = 424-514

# Introduction

SCAT percentiles are used to compare students to the older population to whom the student will be compared. For example, Grade 2 students are compared to a general population of 4th graders and so on, as detailed below:

- Grade 2 is compared to Grade 4
- Grade 3 to Grade 5
- Grade 4 to Grade 6
- Grade 5 to Grade 8
- Grade 6 to Grade 9
- Grade 7 to Grade 12
- Grade 8 to Grade 12

Help your child in preparing for the SCAT test with these full-length practice tests

# Practice Test 1

# Verbal Practice Test

**Directions:**

Each question begins with two words. These two words go together in a certain way. Under them, there are four other pairs of words lettered A, B, C, and D.

Find the lettered pair of words that go together in the same way as the first pair of words.

1. reinforce: stronger
   - A. abound: lesser
   - B. wilt: higher
   - C. large: greater
   - D. erode: weaker

   Answer:

2. erosion: weather
   - A. sublimation: gas
   - B. evaporation: humid
   - C. maceration: liquid
   - D. trail: path

   Answer:

3. braggart: modesty
   - A. fledgling: experience
   - B. candidate: ambition
   - C. invalid: rejection
   - D. selfish: greedy

   Answer:

Grades 6 and above                                  Practice Test 1 Session 1

**4**  barometer: pressure
  A. scale: heavy
  B. anemometer: wind
  C. thermometer: Celsius
  D. meter stick: line

Answer:

**5**  sword: slaughter
  A. scissors: chopping
  B. scalpel: surgery
  C. axe: murder
  D. knife: mother

Answer:

**6**  ecology: environment
  A. cytology: egg
  B. histology: tissues
  C. economy: country
  D. psychology: psychic

Answer:

**7**  coordinated: movement
  A. cooperation: team
  B. prophetic: messenger
  C. articulate: speech
  D. predictive: future

Answer:

**8**  inception: conclusion
  A. departure: arrival
  B. dawn: conception
  C. finish: ending
  D. median: central

Answer:

Grades 6 and above　　　　　　　　　　　　　　　　　　　Practice Test 1 Session 1

**9**  illuminate: light

　　A. remembrance: memory

　　B. elucidate: clarity

　　C. depression: problem

　　D. participate: group

Answer:

**10**  grass: prairie

　　A. flower: vase

　　B. tree: land

　　C. conifer: taiga

　　D. grain: plains

Answer:

**11**  arable: land

　　A. navigable: waterway

　　B. fertile: plant

　　C. shallow: well

　　D. impenetrable: forest

Answer:

**12**  wavelength: amplitude

　　A. timbre: music

　　B. color: hue

　　C. pitch: loudness

　　D. notes: lyrics

Answer:

**13**  medicine: illness

　　A. law: anarchy

　　B. love: treason

　　C. hunger: thirst

　　D. stimulant: sensation

Answer:

**14** paltry: significance
  A. banal: originality
  B. opulent: wealth
  C. plagiarized: work
  D. oblique: familiarity

Answer:

**15** sodden: moist
  A. arid: harsh
  B. wet: liquid
  C. maudlin: sentimental
  D. assertive: alert

Answer:

**16** enlightened: ignorant
  A. aware: smart
  B. elated: despondent
  C. miserable: uncomfortable
  D. lightened: burden

Answer:

**17** sponge: porous
  A. rubber: elastic
  B. solid: matter
  C. wealth: treasure
  D. stone: flexible

Answer:

**18** candid: indirect
  A. frank: strict
  B. honest: untruthful
  C. industrious: hardworking
  D. wicked: harmful

Answer:

**Grades 6 and above**  Practice Test 1 Session 1

**19** archipelago: island

　A. constellation: star

　B. zodiac: Libra

　C. ocean: sea

　D. continent: region

Answer:

**20** dictionary: definition

　A. encyclopedia: spelling

　B. directory: address

　C. thesaurus: flag

　D. atlas: planet

Answer:

**21** condemned: execution

　A. student: graduation

　B. performance: exhibition

　C. elected: inauguration

　D. study: dismissal

Answer:

**22** royalty: author

　A. wage: salary

　B. dividend: stockholder

　C. interest: cashier

　D. bill: customer

Answer:

**23** textbook: lesson plan

　A. brush: nail

　B. jacket: sleeves

　C. palette: easel

　D. window: door

Answer:

Grades 6 and above                                Practice Test 1 Session 1

**24** banquet: feast
- A. palace: mansion
- B. hallway: path
- C. heaven: haven
- D. snack: meal

Answer:

**25** fence: boundary
- A. path: ramp
- B. alley: passageway
- C. pedestrian: people
- D. airfield: airplane

Answer:

**26** appealing: attractive
- A. enormous: exciting
- B. admit: confess
- C. interesting: simple
- D. awful: helpful

Answer:

**27** percussion: instrument
- A. delicious: yummy
- B. chocolate: candy
- C. marsupial: mammal
- D. drum: trumpet

Answer:

**28** massive: bulk
- A. ultimate: magnitude
- B. trivial: importance
- C. gigantic: size
- D. anonymous: synonymous

Answer:

Grades 6 and above                                    Practice Test 1 Session 1

**29** allay: suspicion

    A. calm: fear

    B. anger: mad

    C. forgive: acceptance

    D. happy: thankful

Answer:

**30** segregate: unify

    A. approach: propose

    B. congeal: solidify

    C. ascent: climb

    D. repair: damage

Answer:

**31** monkey: primate

    A. honeybee: hive

    B. moose: mouse

    C. opossum: marsupial

    D. kitten: young

Answer:

**32** ascent: climb

    A. famous: obscure

    B. recession: withdrawal

    C. principle: living

    D. passage: message

Answer:

**33** cottontail: rabbit

    A. persimmon: berry

    B. wing: butterfly

    C. tusk: elephant

    D. carrot: bunny

Answer:

| Grades 6 and above | Practice Test 1 Session 1 |

**34** shuttlecock: badminton

    A. ring: volleyball

    B. field: golf

    C. rook: chess

    D. cushion: table

Answer:

**35** captive: freedom

    A. lawless: order

    B. ledger: account

    C. quarry: marble

    D. ponder: think

Answer:

**36** miser: charitable

    A. authoritarian: lenient

    B. teacher: studious

    C. virtuoso: expert

    D. doctor: empathetic

Answer:

**37** turncoat: traitor

    A. scamp: rogue

    B. pillow: blanket

    C. battle: history

    D. chatter: flutter

Answer:

**38** minuscule: small

    A. wicked: witch

    B. egregious: bad

    C. expensive: cheap

    D. mountain: tall

Answer:

Grades 6 and above

Practice Test 1 Session 1

**39** bolt: leave

- **A.** hive: honey
- **B.** truck: fleet
- **C.** pounce: approach
- **D.** glance: stare

Answer:

**40** kennel: dog

- **A.** cub: kangaroo
- **B.** aerie: bird
- **C.** drone: bee
- **D.** lumber: bear

Answer:

**41** haiku: poem

- **A.** fairytale: adventure
- **B.** fable: story
- **C.** legend: urban
- **D.** music: song

Answer:

**42** secret: furtive

- **A.** vamp: shoe
- **B.** sloth: action
- **C.** audible: resonant
- **D.** babble: speak

Answer:

**43** clumsy: botch

- **A.** lazy: shirk
- **B.** strict: pamper
- **C.** clever: smart
- **D.** drip: gush

Answer:

**44** entice: repel

    A. lubricate: grease

    B. implore: entreat

    C. flourish: fade

    D. notorious: fallible

Answer:

**45** churn: butter

    A. median: highway

    B. press: wine

    C. obstacle: swerve

    D. lightweight: boxer

Answer:

**46** belittle: disparage

    A. reduce: jeopardize

    B. danger: safety

    C. satisfy: frustrate

    D. deride: ridicule

Answer:

**47** fragment: merge

    A. engage: cooperate

    B. splinter: join

    C. mend: repair

    D. loosen: detach

Answer:

**48** homogeneous: kind

    A. diverse: similarity

    B. contemporary: time

    C. guide: direct

    D. heterogeneous: uniformity

Answer:

Grades 6 and above  Practice Test 1 Session 1

**49** careful: cautious

A. boastful: arrogant

B. humble: gullible

C. joyful: wonderful

D. careless: suspicious

Answer:

**50** secretly: openly

A. impolitely: rudely

B. cheerfully: mirthfully

C. luckily: fortunately

D. silently: noisily

Answer:

**51** hedonist: pleasure

A. philanthropist: plant

B. physiologist: mind

C. purist: tradition

D. scientist: past

Answer:

**52** fret: worry

A. concise: discursive

B. brew: contrive

C. particular: ordinary

D. comfort: bother

Answer:

**53** editorial: newspaper

A. shallot: onion

B. rule: verdict

C. salutation: letter

D. gamble: money

Answer:

Grades 6 and above                                    Practice Test 1 Session 1

**54** platoon: soldier

   A. cement: rock

   B. mandible: jaw

   C. knight: horse

   D. purse: money

Answer:

**55** famine: malnutrition

   A. eruption: volcano

   B. drought: water

   C. corruption: poverty

   D. disease: stroke

Answer:

# Optional Break

# Quantitative Practice Test

### Directions:

Each question given below has two parts. One part is column A, the other part is column B. You must find out if one part is greater than the other, or if the parts are equal, you will choose one answer.

A. If the part in column A is greater

B. If the part in column B is greater

C. The two parts are equal

D. If the relationship cannot be determined from the information given.

**Question 1**

| Column A | Column B |
| --- | --- |
| $0.540 + 0.004$ | $0.054 + 0.400$ |

Answer:

**Question 2**

| Column A | Column B |
| --- | --- |
| $|-38|$ | $|38|$ |

Answer:

**Question 3**

| Column A | Column B |
| --- | --- |
| The value of $a$ if $2a \cdot 1 = 15$ | The value of $a$ if $2a + 1 = 13$ |

Answer:

Grades 6 and above    Practice Test 1 Session 2

## Question 4

| Column A | Column B |
|---|---|
| The value of a number if 4 times the number is 4. | The value of a number if 5 times the number is 5. |

Answer:

## Question 5

| Column A | Column B |
|---|---|
| $45 \times 40$ | $(45 \times 5) + (45 \times 35)$ |

Answer:

## Question 6

| Column A | Column B |
|---|---|
| $-12 + (-3)$ | $-12 - 3$ |

Answer:

## Question 7

| Column A | Column B |
|---|---|
| $k < 6$ $k$ | 6 |

Answer:

## Question 8

| Column A | Column B |
|---|---|
| $4^8$ | $20^4$ |

Answer:

## Question 9

| Column A | Column B |
| --- | --- |
| 30% | $\dfrac{5}{7}$ |

Answer:

## Question 10

| Column A | Column B |
| --- | --- |
| $\dfrac{1}{4} \times \dfrac{3}{9} \times \dfrac{7}{2}$ | $\dfrac{1}{9} \times \dfrac{3}{4} \times \dfrac{7}{2}$ |

Answer:

## Question 11

| Column A | Column B |
| --- | --- |
| $1 + 4^2 - 2 - 7$ | $(1+4)^2 - 2 - 7$ |

Answer:

## Question 12

| Column A | Column B |
| --- | --- |
| $x > 0$, $6\sqrt{x}$ where $x$ is natural number. | $x > 0$, $\sqrt{2x}$ where $x$ is natural number. |

Answer:

## Question 13

| Column A | Column B |
| --- | --- |
| $\dfrac{1}{4}$ of $x$ | 26% of $x$ |

Answer:

**Grades 6 and above**      Practice Test 1 Session 2

## Question 14

| Column A | Column B |
|---|---|
| $\frac{1}{4}x + \frac{1}{4}x + \frac{1}{4}x + \frac{1}{4}x = 16$, $x$ | $\frac{1}{4}x + \frac{1}{4}x + \frac{1}{4}x + \frac{1}{4}x = 16$, $16$ |

Answer:

## Question 15

| Column A | Column B |
|---|---|
| $a > 1$ and $b > 1$, $b^{(a-1)}$ where $a, b$ are natural numbers. | $a > 1$ and $b > 1$, $b^{-a}$ where $a, b$ are natural numbers. |

Answer:

## Question 16

| Column A | Column B |
|---|---|
| 29 days | February month |

Answer:

## Question 17

| Column A | Column B |
|---|---|
| $x > y > 0$, $-\frac{x}{xy}$ where $x, y$ are natural numbers. | $x > y > 0$, $\frac{x}{xy}$ where $x, y$ are natural numbers. |

Answer:

## Question 18

| Column A | Column B |
|---|---|
| $1 + \frac{1}{30}$ | $\frac{8}{10} - \frac{7}{100}$ |

Answer:

18

## Question 19

| Column A | Column B |
|---|---|
| $(a^5)^2$ | $a^5 a^5$ |

Answer:

## Question 20

| Column A | Column B |
|---|---|
| The value of $k(x)$ in the equation below, when $x = 5$  $k(x) = 4x^4$ | The value of $k(x)$ in the equation below, when $x = 43$  $k(x) = \dfrac{x - 43}{5}$ |

Answer:

## Question 21

| Column A | Column B |
|---|---|
| The line $y = 5x + 5$ contains the point $(-6, y)$.  The $y$-coordinate for the point | The line $y = 5x + 5$ contains the point $(x, -6)$.  The $x$-coordinate for the point |

Answer:

## Question 22

| Column A | Column B |
|---|---|
| $a > 0$ and $b > 0$, $\sqrt{a} - \sqrt{b}$ where $a, b$ are natural numbers. | $a > 0$ and $b > 0$, $\sqrt{a + b}$ where $a, b$ are natural numbers. |

Answer:

## Question 23

| Column A | Column B |
|---|---|
| Andrew is driving at a steady rate of 60 miles per hour. Find the number of minutes it will take Andrew to drive 30 miles. | 30 minutes |

Answer:

## Question 24

| Column A | Column B |
|---|---|
| $\{x,y\}$ represents the remainder when $x$ is divided by $y$, $\{5^5, 10\}$ | $\{x,y\}$ represents the remainder when $x$ is divided by $y$, $\{10^5, 5\}$ |

Answer:

## Question 25

| Column A | Column B |
|---|---|
| $x, y, z,$ and $m$ are positive integers. $x = \frac{1}{5}m$ and $y = \frac{4}{5}m$ and $z = \frac{10}{9}y$ $x$ | $x, y, z,$ and $m$ are positive integers. $x = \frac{1}{5}m$ and $y = \frac{4}{5}m$ and $z = \frac{10}{9}y$ $z$ |

Answer:

## Question 26

| Column A | Column B |
|---|---|
| The greatest odd number less than 49 | The least odd number greater than 47 |

Answer:

Grades 6 and above  Practice Test 1 Session 2

**Question 27**

| Column A | Column B |
|---|---|
| $\sqrt{\dfrac{13}{2}}$ | $\sqrt{\dfrac{4}{\sqrt{4}}}$ |

Answer:

**Question 28**

| Column A | Column B |
|---|---|
| A distance of 200 meters | A distance of $\dfrac{50}{200}$ kilometer |

Answer:

**Question 29**

| Column A | Column B |
|---|---|
| $k < 0$, $6k$ where $k$ is an integer. | $k < 0$, $k^3$ where $k$ is an integer. |

Answer:

**Question 30**

| Column A | Column B |
|---|---|
| 5 hours 25 minutes <br> +3 hours 15 minutes | 7 hours 20 minutes <br> −         35 minutes |

Answer:

**Question 31**

| Column A | Column B |
|---|---|
| $(-12)^{10}$ | $(-22)^{11}$ |

Answer:

**Grades 6 and above**                  Practice Test 1 Session 2

### Question 32

| Column A | Column B |
| --- | --- |
| $(a^2)^3$ where $a$ is a natural number. | $\sqrt{a^9}$ where $a$ is a natural number. |

Answer:

### Question 33

| Column A | Column B |
| --- | --- |
| The product of the integers from $-2$ to $5$. | The product of the integers from $-1$ to $4$. |

Answer:

### Question 34

| Column A | Column B |
| --- | --- |
| $\dfrac{4x+36}{4}$ | $x+9$ |

Answer:

### Question 35

| Column A | Column B |
| --- | --- |
| .12 | .098 |

Answer:

### Question 36

| Column A | Column B |
| --- | --- |
| $3.25 \times 10^4$ | $32{,}500{,}000 \div 10^2$ |

Answer:

## Question 37

| Column A | Column B |
|---|---|
| $|y-9|$ | $|9-y|$ |

Answer:

## Question 38

| Column A | Column B |
|---|---|
| A class used 90 packages of cheese to make pizzas. Each pizza used $\frac{2}{3}$ a package of cheese. Find the number of pizzas they made. | 50 |

Answer:

## Question 39

| Column A | Column B |
|---|---|
| $a = \frac{2}{3}$ and $b = \frac{4}{5}$, $\frac{a}{b}$ | $a = \frac{2}{3}$ and $b = \frac{4}{5}$, $\frac{b}{a}$ |

Answer:

## Question 40

| Column A | Column B |
|---|---|
| $\frac{3}{2} \times \frac{7}{4} \times \frac{1}{2}$ | $\frac{1}{4} \times \frac{7}{2} \times \frac{3}{2}$ |

Answer:

Grades 6 and above

Practice Test 1 Session 2

## Question 41

| Column A | Column B |
|---|---|
| $2 + 8^2 - 3 - 5$ | $(2+8)^2 - 3 - 5$ |

Answer:

## Question 42

| Column A | Column B |
|---|---|
| $x > 0$, $-5\sqrt{x}$ where $x$ is a natural number. | $x > 0$, $\sqrt{3x}$ where $x$ is a natural number. |

Answer:

## Question 43

| Column A | Column B |
|---|---|
| $\frac{1}{5}x + \frac{1}{5}x + \frac{1}{5}x + \frac{1}{5}x + \frac{1}{5}x = 20$, $x$ | $\frac{1}{5}x + \frac{1}{5}x + \frac{1}{5}x + \frac{1}{5}x + \frac{1}{5}x = 20$, $20$ |

Answer:

## Question 44

| Column A | Column B |
|---|---|
| $a > 1$ and $b > 1$, $(b+1)^{(a-1)}$ where $a, b$ are natural numbers. | $a > 1$ and $b > 1$, $b^{-a+1}$ where $a, b$ are natural numbers. |

Answer:

## Question 45

| Column A | Column B |
|---|---|
| $a > 0$ and $b > 0$, $2\sqrt{a} + 3\sqrt{b}$ where $a, b$ is natural number. | $a > 0$ and $b > 0$, $5\sqrt{a+b}$ where $a, b$ is natural number. |

Answer:

## Question 46

| Column A | Column B |
| --- | --- |
| Jessie is driving at a steady rate of 50 miles per hour. Find the number of minutes it will take Jessie to drive 25 miles. | 30 minutes |

Answer:

## Question 47

| Column A | Column B |
| --- | --- |
| $\{x,y\}$ represents the remainder when $x$ is divided by $y$, $\{8^5, 4\}$ | $\{x,y\}$ represents the remainder when $x$ is divided by $y$, $\{4^{10}, 8\}$ |

Answer:

## Question 48

| Column A | Column B |
| --- | --- |
| $a, b, c,$ and $m$ are positive integers. $a = \frac{1}{4}m$ and $b = \frac{2}{4}m$ and $c = \frac{7}{4}b$ $b$ | $a, b, c,$ and $m$ are positive integers. $a = \frac{1}{4}m$ and $b = \frac{2}{4}m$ and $c = \frac{7}{4}b$ $c$ |

Answer:

## Question 49

| Column A | Column B |
| --- | --- |
| 8 hours 40 minutes<br>+6 hours 30 minutes | 19 hours 20 minutes<br>−9 hours 50 minutes |

Answer:

**Grades 6 and above**          **Practice Test 1 Session 2**

## Question 50

| Column A | Column B |
|---|---|
| $7.46 \times 10^5$ | $7{,}460{,}000 \div 10^4$ |

Answer:

## Question 51

| Column A | Column B |
|---|---|
| $3|z-5|$ | $3|5-z|$ |

Answer:

## Question 52

| Column A | Column B |
|---|---|
| The value of $f(x)$ in the equation below, when $x = 10$ $$f(x) = 3x^3 - 1$$ | The value of $f(x)$ in the equation below, when $x = 23$ $$f(x) = \frac{5x+10}{5}$$ |

Answer:

## Question 53

| Column A | Column B |
|---|---|
| $a = \dfrac{7}{5}$ and $b = \dfrac{3}{2}$, $\dfrac{a}{b}$ | $a = \dfrac{7}{5}$ and $b = \dfrac{3}{2}$, $\dfrac{b}{a}$ |

Answer:

**Question 54**

| Column A | Column B |
|---|---|
| $0.985 + 0.005$ | $0.895 + 0.500$ |

Answer:

**Question 55**

| Column A | Column B |
|---|---|
| The line $y = -x - 24$ contains the point $(-9, y)$. The $y$-coordinate for the point | The line $y = \frac{2}{3}x - 10$ contains the point $(x, -9)$. The $x$-coordinate for the point |

Answer:

# Answer Key

## Verbal

| # | Ans | # | Ans |
|---|---|---|---|
| 1 | D | 29 | A |
| 2 | C | 30 | D |
| 3 | A | 31 | C |
| 4 | B | 32 | B |
| 5 | B | 33 | A |
| 6 | B | 34 | C |
| 7 | C | 35 | A |
| 8 | A | 36 | A |
| 9 | B | 37 | A |
| 10 | C | 38 | B |
| 11 | A | 39 | C |
| 12 | C | 40 | B |
| 13 | A | 41 | B |
| 14 | A | 42 | C |
| 15 | C | 43 | A |
| 16 | B | 44 | C |
| 17 | A | 45 | B |
| 18 | B | 46 | D |
| 19 | A | 47 | B |
| 20 | B | 48 | B |
| 21 | C | 49 | A |
| 22 | B | 50 | D |
| 23 | C | 51 | C |
| 24 | A | 52 | B |
| 25 | B | 53 | C |
| 26 | B | 54 | B |
| 27 | C | 55 | C |
| 28 | C | | |

## Quantitative

| # | Ans | # | Ans |
|---|---|---|---|
| 1 | A | 29 | B |
| 2 | C | 30 | B |
| 3 | A | 31 | A |
| 4 | C | 32 | A |
| 5 | C | 33 | C |
| 6 | C | 34 | C |
| 7 | B | 35 | A |
| 8 | B | 36 | B |
| 9 | B | 37 | C |
| 10 | C | 38 | A |
| 11 | B | 39 | B |
| 12 | A | 40 | C |
| 13 | B | 41 | B |
| 14 | C | 42 | B |
| 15 | A | 43 | C |
| 16 | C | 44 | A |
| 17 | B | 45 | B |
| 18 | A | 46 | C |
| 19 | C | 47 | B |
| 20 | A | 48 | B |
| 21 | B | 49 | A |
| 22 | B | 50 | A |
| 23 | C | 51 | C |
| 24 | B | 52 | A |
| 25 | B | 53 | B |
| 26 | B | 54 | B |
| 27 | A | 55 | B |
| 28 | B | | |

# Answer Key with Explanations

## Verbal

**1** **Answer:** D

**Explanation:** To reinforce is to make stronger and to erode is to make weaker.

**2** **Answer:** C

**Explanation:** A weather causes erosion as liquid causes maceration.

**3** **Answer:** A

**Explanation:** Braggart means arrogant. Thus, someone who is braggart lacks modesty. Fledgling means beginner. Thus, someone who is fledgling lacks experience.

**4** **Answer:** B

**Explanation:** A barometer is used to measure pressure, while an anemometer is used to measure wind pressure.

**5** **Answer:** B

**Explanation:** A sword is used for slaughter and a scalpel is used for surgery.

**6** **Answer:** B

**Explanation:** Ecology is the study of environment and histology is the study of tissues.

**7** **Answer:** C

**Explanation:** A coordinated movement flows well as an articulate speech flows well.

**8** **Answer:** A

**Explanation:** Inception is the beginning of a process and conclusion is the end. Departure is the beginning of a journey and arrival is the end.

**9** **Answer:** B

**Explanation:** To illuminate is to increase light, while to elucidate is to increase clarity.

**10** **Answer:** C

**Explanation:** A grass is a dominant vegetation in prairie and a conifer is a dominant vegetation in taiga.

**11** **Answer:** A

**Explanation:** An arable land is a land suitable for cultivation and a navigable waterway is suitable for sailing.

**12** **Answer:** C

**Explanation:** The pitch of a sound is determined by the wavelength of the sound wave, while the loudness of a sound is determined by the amplitude of the sound wave.

**13** **Answer:** A

**Explanation:** The function of medicine is to prevent or cure illness and the function of law is to prevent or cure anarchy.

14  **Answer:** A

   **Explanation:** Paltry means trashy. Therefore, something paltry lacks significance. Banal means trite. Therefore, something banal lacks originality.

15  **Answer:** C

   **Explanation:** Sodden means soaked. Thus, something sodden is very moist. Maudlin means corny. Thus, someone who is maudlin is very sentimental.

16  **Answer:** B

   **Explanation:** The opposite of enlightened is ignorant and the opposite of elated is despondent.

17  **Answer:** A

   **Explanation:** A characteristic of a sponge is to be porous and a characteristic of a rubber is to be elastic.

18  **Answer:** B

   **Explanation:** Candid means frank or direct. Thus, the opposite of candid is indirect. Honest means truthful. Thus, the opposite of honest is untruthful.

19  **Answer:** A

   **Explanation:** An archipelago is a group of islands as a constellation is a group of stars.

20  **Answer:** B

   **Explanation:** A dictionary is used to look up a definition and a directory is used to look up an address.

21  **Answer:** C

   **Explanation:** An execution takes place after a person is condemned and an inauguration takes place after a person is elected.

22  **Answer:** B

   **Explanation:** A royalty is money paid to an author for the books that have been sold, while a dividend is money paid to a stockholder for the stocks that have performed.

23  **Answer:** C

   **Explanation:** The textbook and lesson plan are things used by a teacher, while the palette and easel are things used by an artist.

24  **Answer:** A

   **Explanation:** A banquet and a feast are both large meals, while a palace and a mansion are both large shelters.

25  **Answer:** B

   **Explanation:** A fence is used to mark a boundary, while an alley is used to mark a passageway.

26  **Answer:** B

   **Explanation:** Appealing is a synonym of attractive and to admit is a synonym of to confess.

27  **Answer:** C

   **Explanation:** A percussion is a type of instrument as a marsupial is a type of mammal.

28   **Answer:** C

   **Explanation:** Something massive has great bulk, while something gigantic has great size.

29   **Answer:** A

   **Explanation:** To allay suspicion is to make suspicion less, while to calm fear is to make fear less.

30   **Answer:** D

   **Explanation:** Segregate means to separate. Thus, to segregate is an antonym of to unify. Repair means fix. Thus, to repair is an antonym of to damage.

31   **Answer:** C

   **Explanation:** A monkey is an example of a primate as an opossum is an example of a marsupial.

32   **Answer:** B

   **Explanation:** Ascent is an act of rising upward. Therefore, to ascent is a synonym of to climb. Recession is the act of ceding back. Therefore, a recession is a synonym of withdrawal.

33   **Answer:** A

   **Explanation:** A cottontail is a type of rabbit and a persimmon is a type of berry.

34   **Answer:** C

   **Explanation:** A shuttlecock is used to play badminton as a rook is a piece used to play chess.

35   **Answer:** A

   **Explanation:** Captive means prisoner. Thus, to be captive is to lack freedom. Lawless means unruly. Thus, to be lawless is to lack order.

36   **Answer:** A

   **Explanation:** A miser is a person who is extremely stingy with money. Therefore, being charitable is not a characteristic of a miser. An authoritarian is a strict person. Therefore, being lenient is not a characteristic of an authoritarian.

37   **Answer:** A

   **Explanation:** Turncoat is a person who switches to an opposing side. Thus, turncoat is another word for traitor. Scamp is a playful young person. Thus, scamp is another word for rogue.

38   **Answer:** B

   **Explanation:** Something that is minuscule is very small and something that is egregious is very bad.

39   **Answer:** C

   **Explanation:** To bolt is to leave suddenly, while to pounce is to approach suddenly.

40   **Answer:** B

   **Explanation:** A kennel houses dogs as an aerie houses birds.

41   **Answer:** B

   **Explanation:** A haiku is a type of poem and a fable is a type of story.

42   **Answer:** C

   **Explanation:** Furtive is more intensely secret and resonant is more intensely audible.

43  **Answer:** A

Explanation: Botch means screw up. Thus, someone who is clumsy may botch a job. Shirk means sneak. Thus, someone who is lazy may shirk work.

44  **Answer:** C

Explanation: Entice means attract. Thus, entice is the opposite of repel. Flourish means thrive. Thus, flourish is the opposite of fade.

45  **Answer:** B

Explanation: A churn is used to make butter, while a press is used to make wine.

46  **Answer:** D

Explanation: To belittle and to disparage are synonyms meaning to criticize. To deride and to ridicule are synonyms meaning to mock.

47  **Answer:** B

Explanation: To fragment means to break up. Thus, to fragment is the opposite of to merge. To splinter means to break up also. Thus, to splinter is the opposite of to join.

48  **Answer:** B

Explanation: Homogeneous things are all of the same kind, while contemporary things are of the same time.

49  **Answer:** A

Explanation: Someone who is careful is cautious, while someone who is boastful is arrogant.

50  **Answer:** D

Explanation: Secretly is the opposite of openly, while silently is the opposite of noisily.

51  **Answer:** C

Explanation: A hedonist is fixated on pleasure, as purist is fixated on tradition.

52  **Answer:** B

Explanation: To fret means to worry and to brew means to contrive.

53  **Answer:** C

Explanation: Editorial is an article that contains the opinions of the publishers. Thus, an editorial is part of a newspaper. Salutation is an expression of greeting. Thus, a salutation is part of a letter.

54  **Answer:** B

Explanation: Platoon is an army. Thus, a soldier is part of a platoon. Mandible is a lower jaw. Thus, a mandible is part of a jaw.

55  **Answer:** C

Explanation: Famine is an extreme scarcity of food. Thus, famine is a cause of malnutrition. Corruption is an illegal behavior by powerful people. Thus, corruption is a cause of poverty.

Grades 6 and above — Practice Test 1 Session 2

# Quantitative

**1**   **Answer:** A

**Explanation:** Column A is $0.544$ whereas column B is $0.454$. Therefore, column A is greater. The correct answer is (A).

**2**   **Answer:** C

**Explanation:** The absolute value of column A is 38 whereas column B is also 38. Therefore, both columns are equal. The correct answer is (C).

**3**   **Answer:** A

**Explanation:** Column A is $2a = 15 \Rightarrow a = 7.5$ whereas column B is $2a + 1 = 13 \Rightarrow 2a = 12 \Rightarrow a = 6$. Therefore, column A is greater. The correct answer is (A).

**4**   **Answer:** C

**Explanation:** Column A is 1 as $1 \times 4 = 4$ whereas column B is 1 as $1 \times 5 = 5$. Therefore, both columns are equal. The correct answer is (C).

**5**   **Answer:** C

**Explanation:** Column A is $45 \times 40$ whereas column B is $(45 \times 5) + (45 \times 35) = 45 \times (5 + 35) = 45 \times 40$. Therefore, both columns are equal. The correct answer is (C).

**6**   **Answer:** C

**Explanation:** Column A is $-12 + (-3) = -12 - 3 = -15$ whereas column B is $-12 - 3 = -15$. Therefore, both columns are equal. The correct answer is (C).

**7**   **Answer:** B

**Explanation:** Column A can be 0, 1, 2, 3, 4, 5 whereas column B is 6. Therefore, column B is greater. The correct answer is (B).

**8**   **Answer:** B

**Explanation:** Column A is $4^8 = 4 \cdot 4 \cdot 4 \cdot 4 \cdot 4 \cdot 4 \cdot 4 \cdot 4 = 65,536$ whereas column B is $20^4 = 20 \cdot 20 \cdot 20 \cdot 20 = 160,000$. Therefore, column B is greater. The correct answer is (B).

**9**   **Answer:** B

**Explanation:** Column A is $30 \times 0.01 = 0.3$ whereas column B is $\dfrac{5}{7} = 0.7142$. Therefore, column B is greater. The correct answer is (B).

**10**   **Answer:** C

**Explanation:** Column A is $\dfrac{1}{4} \times \dfrac{3}{9} \times \dfrac{7}{2} = \dfrac{7}{24} = 0.2916$ whereas column B is $\dfrac{1}{9} \times \dfrac{3}{4} \times \dfrac{7}{2} = \dfrac{7}{24} = 0.2916$. Therefore, both columns are equal. The correct answer is (C).

**11**   **Answer:** B

**Explanation:** Column A is $1 + 4^2 - 2 - 7 = 1 + 16 - 9 = 8$ whereas column B is $(1+4)^2 - 2 - 7 = 5^2 - 9 = 25 - 9 = 16$. Therefore, column B is greater. The correct answer is (B).

**12**   **Answer:** A

**Explanation:** Assume $x = 1$, Column A is 6 whereas column B is $\sqrt{2} = 1.414$. Therefore, column A is greater. The correct answer is (A).

| Grades 6 and above | Practice Test 1 Session 2 |

**13** **Answer: B**

**Explanation:** Column A is $\frac{1}{4}x = 0.25x$ whereas column B is $\frac{26}{100}x = 0.26x$. Therefore, column B is greater. The correct answer is (B).

**14** **Answer: C**

**Explanation:** Column A is,

$$\frac{1}{4}x + \frac{1}{4}x + \frac{1}{4}x + \frac{1}{4}x = 16$$

$$\frac{1+1+1+1}{4}x = 16$$

$$\frac{4}{4}x = 16$$

$$x = 16$$

whereas column B is also 16. Therefore, both columns are equal. The correct answer is (C).

**15** **Answer: A**

**Explanation:** Assume $a = 2$ and $b = 2$, Column A is $2^{(2-1)} = 2^1 = 2$ whereas column B is $2^{-2} = \frac{1}{4} = 0.25$. Therefore, column A is greater. The correct answer is (A).

**16** **Answer: C**

**Explanation:** As it is known that February month may be 28 or 29 days. Therefore, both columns are equal. The correct answer is (C).

**17** **Answer: B**

**Explanation:** Assume $x = 1$ and $y = 1$, Column A is $-\frac{x}{xy} = -\frac{1}{1 \cdot 1} = -1$ whereas column B is $\frac{x}{xy} = \frac{1}{1 \cdot 1} = 1$.

Therefore, column B is greater. The correct answer is (B).

**18** **Answer: A**

**Explanation:** Column A is $1 + \frac{1}{30} = \frac{30+1}{30} = \frac{31}{30} = 1.033$ whereas column B is $\frac{8}{10} - \frac{7}{100} = \frac{80-7}{100} = \frac{73}{100} = 0.73$.

Therefore, column A is greater. The correct answer is (A).

**19** **Answer: C**

**Explanation:** Column A is $(a^5)^2 = a^{5 \cdot 2} = a^{10}$ whereas column B is $a^5 a^5 = a^{5+5} = a^{10}$. Therefore, both columns are equal. The correct answer is (C).

**20** **Answer: A**

**Explanation:** Column A is $k(5) = 4(5)^4 = 2500$ whereas column B is $k(43) = \frac{43-43}{5} = 0$. Therefore, column A is greater. The correct answer is (A).

**21** **Answer: B**

**Explanation:** Column A is $y = 5(-6) + 5 = -25$ whereas column B is $-6 = 5x + 5 \Rightarrow 5x = -11 \Rightarrow x = -2.2$. Therefore, column B is greater. The correct answer is (B).

**22** **Answer: B**

**Explanation:** Assume $a = 1$ and $b = 1$, Column A is $\sqrt{1} - \sqrt{1} = 1 - 1 = 0$ whereas column B is $\sqrt{1+1} = \sqrt{2} = 1.414$. Therefore, column B is greater. The correct answer is (B).

**Grades 6 and above**                                          **Practice Test 1 Session 2**

**23**    **Answer:** C

        **Explanation:** The time taken by Andrew to drive 30 miles is 30 minutes as Andrew is driving 60 miles in 60 minutes. Therefore, both columns are equal. The correct answer is (C).

**24**    **Answer:** B

        **Explanation:** Column A is $\frac{5^5}{10} = \frac{3,125}{10} = 312.5$ whereas column B is $\frac{10^5}{5} = \frac{100,000}{5} = 20,000$. Therefore, column B is greater. The correct answer is (B).

**25**    **Answer:** B

        **Explanation:** Assume $m = 1$ and $y = 1$, Column A is $x = \frac{1}{5}(1) = 0.2$ whereas column B is $z = \frac{10}{9}(1) = 1.11$. Therefore, column B is greater. The correct answer is (B).

**26**    **Answer:** B

        **Explanation:** Column A is 47 whereas column B is 49. Therefore, column B is greater. The correct answer is (B).

**27**    **Answer:** A

        **Explanation:** Column A is $\sqrt{\frac{13}{2}} = \sqrt{6.5}$ whereas column B is $\sqrt{\frac{4}{\sqrt{4}}} = \frac{2}{\sqrt{2}} = \sqrt{2}$. Therefore, column A is greater. The correct answer is (A).

**28**    **Answer:** B

        **Explanation:** As it is known that $1000m = 1$ kilometer. Column A is 200 meters whereas column B is 250 meters as $\frac{50}{200} \times 1000 = 250$. Therefore, column B is greater. The correct answer is (B).

**29**    **Answer:** B

        **Explanation:** Assume $k = -1$, Column A is $6k = 6(-1) = -6$ whereas column B is $k^3 = (-1)^3 = -1$. Therefore, column B is greater. The correct answer is (B).

**30**    **Answer:** B

        **Explanation:** As it is known that 1 hour is equal to 60 minutes. Column A is,

              5 hours 25 minutes
            +3 hours 15 minutes
             8 hours 40 minutes

        whereas column B is,

              6 hours 80 minutes
                       −      35 minutes.
             6 hours 45 minutes

        Therefore, column A is greater. The correct answer is (A).

**31**    **Answer:** A

        **Explanation:** Column A is some positive number whereas column B is some negative number as even power gives positive quantity and odd power gives negative quantity. Therefore, column A is greater. The correct answer is (A).

Grades 6 and above | Practice Test 1 Session 2

32  **Answer:** A
**Explanation:** Column A is $\left(a^2\right)^3 = a^{2 \cdot 3} = a^6$ whereas column B is $\sqrt{a^9} = a^{9/2} = a^{4.5}$. Therefore, column A is greater. The correct answer is (A).

33  **Answer:** C
**Explanation:** Column A is $-2(-1)0(1)(2)(3)(4)(5) = 0$ whereas column B is $(-1)0(1)(2)(3)(4) = 0$. Therefore, both columns are equal. The correct answer is (C).

34  **Answer:** C
**Explanation:** Column A is $\dfrac{4x+36}{4} = \dfrac{4(x+9)}{4} = x+9$ which is equal to column B. Therefore, both columns are equal. The correct answer is (C).

35  **Answer:** A
**Explanation:** Column A is greater than column B. The correct answer is (A).

36  **Answer:** B
**Explanation:** Column A is $325 \times 10^4 \times 10^{-2} = 32,500$ whereas column B is
$32,500,000 \div 10^2 = \dfrac{325 \times 10^5}{10^2} = 325,000$. Therefore, column B is greater. The correct answer is (B).

37  **Answer:** C
**Explanation:** The absolute value of column A is $|y-9| = y-9$ whereas column B is $|9-y| = |(-1)(y-9)| = y-9$. Therefore, both columns are equal. The correct answer is (C).

38  **Answer:** A
**Explanation:** Column A is $\dfrac{2}{3}(90) = 2 \cdot 30 = 60$ whereas column B is 50. Therefore, column A is greater. The correct answer is (A).

39  **Answer:** B
**Explanation:** Column A is $\dfrac{2/3}{4/5} = \dfrac{2 \cdot 5}{3 \cdot 4} = \dfrac{5}{6} = 0.8333$ whereas column B is $\dfrac{6}{5} = 1.2$ Therefore, column B is greater. The correct answer is (B).

40  **Answer:** C
**Explanation:** Column A is $\dfrac{3}{2} \times \dfrac{7}{4} \times \dfrac{1}{2} = \dfrac{21}{16} = 1.3125$ whereas column B is $\dfrac{1}{4} \times \dfrac{7}{2} \times \dfrac{3}{2} = \dfrac{21}{16} = 1.3125$. Therefore, both columns are equal. The correct answer is (C).

41  **Answer:** B
**Explanation:** Column A is $2 + 8^2 - 3 - 5 = 2 + 64 - 8 = 58$ whereas column B is $(2+8)^2 - 3 - 5 = 100 - 8 = 92$. Therefore, column B is greater. The correct answer is (B).

42  **Answer:** B
**Explanation:** Assume $x = 2$, Column A is $-5\sqrt{2}$ whereas column B is $\sqrt{3 \cdot 2} = \sqrt{6}$. Therefore, column B is greater. The correct answer is (B).

**Grades 6 and above**                                                                            **Practice Test 1 Session 2**

---

**43**   Answer: C

Explanation: Column A is,

$$\frac{1}{5}x + \frac{1}{5}x + \frac{1}{5}x + \frac{1}{5}x + \frac{1}{5}x = 20$$
$$\frac{1+1+1+1+1}{5}x = 20$$
$$\frac{5}{5}x = 20$$
$$x = 20$$

whereas column B is also 20. Therefore, both columns are equal. The correct answer is (C).

**44**   Answer: A

Explanation: Assume $a = 4$ and $b = 4$, Column A is $(4+1)^{(4-1)} = 5^3 = 125$ whereas column B is $4^{-4+1} = \frac{1}{64}$. Therefore, column A is greater. The correct answer is (A).

**45**   Answer: B

Explanation: Assume $a = 4$ and $b = 4$, Column A is $2\sqrt{a} + 3\sqrt{b} = 2\sqrt{4} + 3\sqrt{4} = 4 + 6 = 10$ whereas column B is $5\sqrt{a+b} = 5\sqrt{4+4} = 5\sqrt{8} = 10\sqrt{2}$. Therefore, column B is greater. The correct answer is (B).

**46**   Answer: C

Explanation: The time taken by Jessie to drive 25 miles is 30 minutes as Jessie is driving 50 miles in 60 minutes. Therefore, both columns are equal. The correct answer is (C).

**47**   Answer: B

Explanation: Column A is $\dfrac{8^5}{4} = \dfrac{(2^3)^5}{2^2} = \dfrac{2^{15}}{2^2} = 2^{13}$ whereas column B is $\dfrac{4^{10}}{8} = \dfrac{(2^2)^{10}}{2^3} = \dfrac{2^{20}}{2^3} = 2^{17}$.

Therefore, column B is greater. The correct answer is (B).

**48**   Answer: B

Explanation: Assume $m = 2$, Column A is $b = \dfrac{2}{4}(2) = 1$ whereas column B is $c = \dfrac{7}{4}(1) = 1.75$.

Therefore, column B is greater. The correct answer is (B).

**49**   Answer: A

Explanation: As it is known that 1 hour is equal to 60 minutes. Column A is,

```
  8 hours 40 minutes
 +6 hours 30 minutes
 15 hours 10 minutes
```

whereas column B is,

```
 18 hours 80 minutes
 −9 hours 50 minutes
  9 hours 30 minutes
```

Therefore, column A is greater. The correct answer is (A).

**Grades 6 and above**                                                                   **Practice Test 1 Session 2**

50    **Answer:** A

      **Explanation:** Column A is $7.46 \times 10^5 = 746 \times 10^{-2} \times 10^5 = 746,000$ whereas column B is

      $7,460,000 \div 10^4 = \dfrac{746 \times 10^4}{10^4} = 746$. Therefore, column A is greater. The correct answer is (A).

51    **Answer:** C

      **Explanation:** The absolute value of column A is $3|z-5| = 3(z-5)$ whereas column B is

      $3|5-z| = 3|(-1)(z-5)| = 3(z-5)$. Therefore, both columns are equal. The correct answer is (C).

52    **Answer:** A

      **Explanation:** Column A is $f(10) = 3(10)^3 - 1 = 2999$ whereas column B is $f(23) = \dfrac{5(23)+10}{5} = \dfrac{125}{5} = 25$.

      Therefore, column A is greater. The correct answer is (A).

53    **Answer:** B

      **Explanation:** Column A is $\dfrac{7/5}{3/2} = \dfrac{2 \cdot 7}{3 \cdot 5} = \dfrac{14}{15}$ whereas column B is $\dfrac{15}{14}$. Therefore, column B is greater. The correct answer is (B).

54    **Answer:** B

      **Explanation:** Column A is $0.990$ whereas column B is $1.395$. Therefore, column B is greater. The correct answer is (B).

55    **Answer:** B

      **Explanation:** Column A is $y = -(-9) - 24 = -15$ whereas column B is $(-9) = \dfrac{2}{3}x - 10 \Rightarrow -27 = 2x - 30 \Rightarrow$

      $x = 1.5$. Therefore, column B is greater. The correct answer is (B).

# Practice Test 2

# Verbal Practice Test

**Directions:**

Each question begins with two words. These two words go together in a certain way. Under them, there are four other pairs of words lettered A, B, C, and D.

Find the lettered pair of words that go together in the same way as the first pair of words.

1. chronological: time
    A. variable: value
    B. ordinal: place
    C. historical: artifact
    D. virtual: truth

Answer:

2. rain: sodden
    A. frost: transparent
    B. dust: radiant
    C. soot: grimy
    D. pall: gaudy

Answer:

3. cottage: mansion
    A. falls: mountain
    B. camp: tent
    C. pond: lake
    D. hamlet: house

Answer:

Grades 6 and above · Practice Test 2 Session 1

**4** conciliate: gentle
   A. ameliorate: worse
   B. retaliate: vengeful
   C. iterate: illiterate
   D. ruminate: lovable

Answer:

**5** satire: parody
   A. attire: beauty
   B. perfidy: treachery
   C. sapphire: jewelry
   D. retire: profession

Answer:

**6** phonetics: language
   A. mnemonics: memory
   B. graphics: graph
   C. lunatic: moon
   D. aquatic: shark

Answer:

**7** wildcat: oil
   A. hunt: forest
   B. bobcat: game
   C. forage: food
   D. lock: canal

Answer:

**8** didactic: teacher
   A. machine: mechanic
   B. debate: speaker
   C. histrionic: actor
   D. historic: history

Answer:

**Grades 6 and above**                                         Practice Test 2 Session 1

**9**   mosaic: tile

   A. art: color

   B. decoration: picture

   C. engrave: name

   D. film: frame

Answer:

**10**   fret: guitar

   A. wind: flute

   B. valve: trumpet

   C. ukulele: violin

   D. beat: drum

Answer:

**11**   condensation: humidity

   A. evaporation: cloud

   B. erosion: rainfall

   C. precipitation: atmosphere

   D. eruption: volcano

Answer:

**12**   abacus: calculation

   A. thermometer: degree

   B. calculator: number

   C. protractor: fraction

   D. sextant: navigation

Answer:

**13**   appendix: book

   A. definition: dictionary

   B. epilogue: play

   C. map: atlas

   D. paper: notebook

Answer:

Grades 6 and above         Practice Test 2 Session 1

**14** keen: mourning

　A. whoop: exuberance

　B. sleep: evening

　C. smile: cheering

　D. lunch: afternoon

Answer:

**15** raconteur: narrate

　A. clown: laugh

　B. host: entertain

　C. raccoon: animal

　D. audience: applause

Answer:

**16** compass: direction

　A. thread: height

　B. scale: heavy

　C. odometer: mileage

　D. microscope: star

Answer:

**17** psychologist: neurosis

　A. dermatologist: fracture

　B. orthopedist: rash

　C. ophthalmologist: cataract

　D. oncologist: measles

Answer:

**18** ream: paper

　A. coal: fire

　B. acre: plow

　C. skein: yarn

　D. lumber: tree

Answer:

**19** monk: devoted

    A. rover: wanderlust

    B. explorer: contentment

    C. priest: gullible

    D. doctor: fallible

Answer:

**20** horror: fear

    A. mimicry: tears

    B. fallacy: dismay

    C. slapstick: laughter

    D. genre: mystery

Answer:

**21** phobic: fearful

    A. cautious: emotional

    B. asinine: silly

    C. shy: confident

    D. finicky: thoughtful

Answer:

**22** feral: tame

    A. repetitive: recurrent

    B. repentant: honorable

    C. ephemeral: immortal

    D. rancid: rational

Answer:

**23** frown: displeasure

    A. fidget: restlessness

    B. hunch: boastful

    C. squirm: comfortable

    D. strut: shy

Answer:

Grades 6 and above                                    Practice Test 2 Session 1

**24** laceration: skin
  A. adhesion: tape
  B. wound: scar
  C. perforation: seal
  D. lactation: milk

Answer:

**25** skeptical: doubt
  A. gullible: easy
  B. narcissistic: selfish
  C. hysterical: hilarious
  D. choleric: anger

Answer:

**26** satin: smooth
  A. wood: volatile
  B. shatter: brittle
  C. treacle: viscous
  D. mirror: rough

Answer:

**27** ambition: success
  A. terror: trepidation
  B. avarice: money
  C. respect: disfavor
  D. profession: career

Answer:

**28** probity: guile
  A. industry: laziness
  B. felicity: happiness
  C. decorum: propriety
  D. fortunate: providential

Answer:

**Grades 6 and above**　　　　　　　　　　　　　　　Practice Test 2 Session 1

**29** badger: annoy

    A. reconcile: disharmonize

    B. ancient: modern

    C. quarrel: dispute

    D. attack: defend

Answer:

**30** display: hide

    A. dither: settle

    B. corrupt: decadent

    C. bother: aggravate

    D. dismay: concern

Answer:

**31** manacle: hands

    A. fetter: feet

    B. fodder: domestic

    C. shin: waist

    D. stock: plant

Answer:

**32** revolver: gun

    A. bullet: pellet

    B. vest: wear

    C. scimitar: saber

    D. pestle: mortar

Answer:

**33** license: marriage

    A. couple: wedding

    B. receipt: purchase

    C. menu: restaurant

    D. diploma: school

Answer:

Grades 6 and above                                              Practice Test 2 Session 1

**34** interest: obsession

  A. mood: feeling

  B. payment: bill

  C. loan: instalment

  D. dream: fantasy

Answer:

**35** sound: cacophony

  A. smell: stench

  B. touch: massage

  C. speech: oration

  D. notes: music

Answer:

**36** inventor: imaginative

  A. aviator: licensed

  B. moderator: vicious

  C. professor: erudite

  D. scientist: wealthy

Answer:

**37** worship: reverence

  A. rage: enthusiasm

  B. intensity: color

  C. eminence: lowland

  D. religious: impious

Answer:

**38** partisan: biased

  A. finite: limited

  B. dogged: amenable

  C. balanced: deranged

  D. hurtful: harmless

Answer:

**Grades 6 and above**                                      Practice Test 2 Session 1

**39** conductor: orchestra

    **A.** painter: house

    **B.** jockey: mount

    **C.** driver: tractor

    **D.** skipper: crew

**Answer:**

**40** frond: palm

    **A.** quill: porcupine

    **B.** tusk: alligator

    **C.** thorn: apple

    **D.** blade: fern

**Answer:**

**41** sneer: contempt

    **A.** admit: confess

    **B.** glower: anger

    **C.** chide: reprimand

    **D.** glare: happiness

**Answer:**

**42** dappled: spots

    **A.** smudge: stain

    **B.** letter: symbol

    **C.** riddled: holes

    **D.** square: quadrilateral

**Answer:**

**43** dilate: size

    **A.** disseminate: break

    **B.** promulgate: publish

    **C.** announce: information

    **D.** proliferate: number

**Answer:**

Grades 6 and above                                      Practice Test 2 Session 1

**44** arena: conflict

    A. building: fight

    B. forum: debate

    C. stadium: examinations

    D. gymnasium: camp

Answer:

**45** sham: hoax

    A. brig: prison

    B. ferry: passenger

    C. juggle: undeceive

    D. linger: hurry

Answer:

**46** praise: insult

    A. mumble: enunciate

    B. broadcast: annunciate

    C. upbraid: rant

    D. umbrage: offense

Answer:

**47** baste: cooking

    A. pinch: snitch

    B. mulch: gardening

    C. paste: sticking

    D. thread: sewing

Answer:

**48** reprove: chide

    A. improve: development

    B. approve: sanction

    C. testify: refuse

    D. cancel: continue

Answer:

**49** leaden: heavy

   A. ravenous: hungry
   B. feather: light
   C. fleet: slow
   D. leather: skin

Answer:

**50** garner: earn

   A. gamble: money
   B. gardener: plant
   C. gather: spend
   D. garble: distort

Answer:

**51** limp: injury

   A. lump: stumble
   B. incarceration: conviction
   C. inflammation: redness
   D. itch: disease

Answer:

**52** sectarian: sect

   A. partisan: cause
   B. believer: skeptic
   C. priest: church
   D. secretary: company

Answer:

**53** dirge: funeral

   A. chain: letter
   B. bell: church
   C. jingle: commercial
   D. hymn: concert

Answer:

54. petrify: stone
    A. inscription: paper
    B. magnify: glass
    C. amplify: speaker
    D. ossify: bone

Answer:

55. mammal: placental
    A. drama: melodrama
    B. weather: spring
    C. reptile: cannibal
    D. animal: plant

Answer:

# Optional Break

# Quantitative Practice Test

### Directions:

Each question given below has two parts. One part is column A, the other part is column B. You must find out if one part is greater than the other, or if the parts are equal, you will choose one answer.

A. If the part in column A is greater

B. If the part in column B is greater

C. The two parts are equal

D. If the relationship cannot be determined from the information given.

**Question 1**

| Column A | Column B |
| --- | --- |
| $2 + 6^2 - 5 - 9$ | $(2+6)^2 - 5 - 9$ |

Answer:

**Question 2**

| Column A | Column B |
| --- | --- |
| $y > 1$, $9\sqrt{y}$ where $y$ is natural number. | $y > 1$, $\sqrt{9y}$ where $y$ is natural number. |

Answer:

**Question 3**

| Column A | Column B |
| --- | --- |
| $\frac{3}{4}$ of $z$ | 54% of $z$ |

Answer:

## Question 4

| Column A | Column B |
|---|---|
| $\frac{1}{5}y + \frac{1}{5}y + \frac{1}{5}y + \frac{1}{5}y + \frac{1}{5}y = 20$, $y$ | $\frac{1}{5}y + \frac{1}{5}y + \frac{1}{5}y + \frac{1}{5}y + \frac{1}{5}y = 20$, $20$ |

Answer:

## Question 5

| Column A | Column B |
|---|---|
| $a > 1$ and $b > 1$, $(a-1)^{(b)}$ where $a$, $b$ are natural numbers. | $a > 1$ and $b > 1$, $a^b$ where $a$, $b$ are natural numbers. |

Answer:

## Question 6

| Column A | Column B |
|---|---|
| 29 days | February month |

Answer:

## Question 7

| Column A | Column B |
|---|---|
| $x > y > 1$, $\frac{x^2}{x+y^2}$ where $x$, $y$ are natural numbers. | $x > y > 1$, $\frac{x^2}{x-y^2}$ where $x$, $y$ are natural numbers. |

Answer:

# Grades 6 and above — Practice Test 2 Session 2

## Question 8

| Column A | Column B |
|---|---|
| $5 + \dfrac{15}{60}$ | $\dfrac{12}{100} - \dfrac{7}{500}$ |

Answer:

## Question 9

| Column A | Column B |
|---|---|
| $\left(b^7\right)^4$ | $b^7 b^7 b^7 b^7$ |

Answer:

## Question 10

| Column A | Column B |
|---|---|
| The value of $f(x)$ in the equation below, when $x = 6$  $f(x) = -10x^3$ | The value of $f(x)$ in the equation below, when $x = 40$  $f(x) = -\dfrac{x-4}{5}$ |

Answer:

## Question 11

| Column A | Column B |
|---|---|
| $0.350 + 0.003$ | $0.035 + 0.300$ |

Answer:

## Question 12

| Column A | Column B |
|---|---|
| $\lvert -99 \rvert$ | $\lvert 99 \rvert$ |

Answer:

# Grades 6 and above — Practice Test 2 Session 2

## Question 13

| Column A | Column B |
|---|---|
| The value of $k$ if $3k \cdot 1 = 18$ | The value of $k$ if $3k + 1 = 18$ |

Answer:

## Question 14

| Column A | Column B |
|---|---|
| The value of a number if 9 times the number is 9. | The value of a number if 7 times the number is 7. |

Answer:

## Question 15

| Column A | Column B |
|---|---|
| $35 \times 30$ | $(35 \times 15) + (35 \times 15)$ |

Answer:

## Question 16

| Column A | Column B |
|---|---|
| $-23 + (-6)$ | $-23 - 6$ |

Answer:

## Question 17

| Column A | Column B |
|---|---|
| $x < 9$ $x$ | $9$ |

Answer:

58

**Grades 6 and above**  Practice Test 2 Session 2

## Question 18

| Column A | Column B |
|---|---|
| $5^4$ | $10^5$ |

Answer:

## Question 19

| Column A | Column B |
|---|---|
| 50% | $\dfrac{12}{15}$ |

Answer:

## Question 20

| Column A | Column B |
|---|---|
| $\dfrac{2}{9} \times \dfrac{5}{7} \times \dfrac{3}{6}$ | $\dfrac{3}{7} \times \dfrac{2}{6} \times \dfrac{5}{9}$ |

Answer:

## Question 21

| Column A | Column B |
|---|---|
| The line $y = -3x - 10$ contains the point $(-4, y)$. | The line $y = -3x - 10$ contains the point $(x, -4)$. |
| The $y$-coordinate for the point | The $x$-coordinate for the point |

Answer:

59

## Question 22

| Column A | Column B |
|---|---|
| $a > 0$ and $b > 0$, $\sqrt{5a^3} - \sqrt{6b^2}$ where $a, b$ are natural numbers. | $a > 0$ and $b > 0$, $\sqrt{5a^3 + 6b^2}$ where $a, b$ are natural numbers. |

Answer:

## Question 23

| Column A | Column B |
|---|---|
| Essa is driving at a steady rate of 50 miles per hour. Find the number of minutes it will take Essa to drive 25 miles. | 30 minutes |

Answer:

## Question 24

| Column A | Column B |
|---|---|
| $\{x, y\}$ represents the remainder when $x$ is divided by $y$, $\{10^4, 40\}$ | $\{x, y\}$ represents the remainder when $x$ is divided by $y$, $\{40^2, 10\}$ |

Answer:

## Question 25

| Column A | Column B |
|---|---|
| $x, y, z,$ and $m$ are positive integers. $x = -\frac{1}{5}m$ and $y = \frac{5}{4}m$ and $z = \frac{7}{10}y$  $y$ | $x, y, z,$ and $m$ are positive integers. $x = -\frac{1}{5}m$ and $y = \frac{5}{4}m$ and $z = \frac{7}{10}y$  $z$ |

Answer:

**Question 26**

| Column A | Column B |
|---|---|
| The greatest odd number less than 63 | The least odd number greater than 61 |

Answer:

**Question 27**

| Column A | Column B |
|---|---|
| $\sqrt{\dfrac{43}{20}}$ | $\sqrt{\dfrac{43}{\sqrt{40}}}$ |

Answer:

**Question 28**

| Column A | Column B |
|---|---|
| A distance of 500 meters | A distance of $\dfrac{50}{500}$ kilometer |

Answer:

**Question 29**

| Column A | Column B |
|---|---|
| $k < 0$, $45k$ where $k$ is an integer. | $k < 0$, $k^3$ where $k$ is an integer. |

Answer:

**Question 30**

| Column A | Column B |
|---|---|
| 6 hours 35 minutes <br> +2 hours 25 minutes | 5 hours 40 minutes <br> −         25 minutes |

Answer:

**Grades 6 and above**  Practice Test 2 Session 2

## Question 31

| Column A | Column B |
|---|---|
| $93.5 \times 10^4$ | $92,100,000 \div 10^4$ |

Answer:

## Question 32

| Column A | Column B |
|---|---|
| $|z - 15|$ | $|15 - z|$ |

Answer:

## Question 33

| Column A | Column B |
|---|---|
| A class used 72 packages of cheese to make pizzas. Each pizza used $\frac{2}{3}$ a package of cheese. Find the number of pizzas they made. | 47 |

Answer:

## Question 34

| Column A | Column B |
|---|---|
| $a = \frac{12}{23}$ and $b = \frac{23}{12}$, $\frac{a}{b}$ | $a = \frac{12}{23}$ and $b = \frac{23}{12}$, $\frac{b}{a}$ |

Answer:

# Question 35

| Column A | Column B |
|---|---|
| $(-13)^{10}$ | $(-21)^{11}$ |

Answer:

# Question 36

| Column A | Column B |
|---|---|
| $(a^5)^4$ where $a$ is natural number. | $\sqrt{a^{19}}$ where $a$ is natural number. |

Answer:

# Question 37

| Column A | Column B |
|---|---|
| The product of the integers from $-1$ to $4$. | The product of the integers from $-3$ to $5$. |

Answer:

# Question 38

| Column A | Column B |
|---|---|
| $\dfrac{9x+63}{9}$ | $x+7$ |

Answer:

# Question 39

| Column A | Column B |
|---|---|
| .24 | .079 |

Answer:

## Question 40

| Column A | Column B |
|---|---|
| $12 + 4^2 - 8 - 7$ | $(12 + 4)^2 - 8 - 7$ |

Answer:

## Question 41

| Column A | Column B |
|---|---|
| $x > 0$, $-42\sqrt{x}$ where $x$ is a natural number. | $x > 0$, $\sqrt{12x}$ where $x$ is a natural number. |

Answer:

## Question 42

| Column A | Column B |
|---|---|
| $\frac{1}{6}z + \frac{1}{6}z + \frac{1}{6}z + \frac{1}{6}z + \frac{1}{6}z + \frac{1}{6}z = 24$, $z$ | $\frac{1}{6}z + \frac{1}{6}z + \frac{1}{6}z + \frac{1}{6}z + \frac{1}{6}z + \frac{1}{6}z = 24$, $24$ |

Answer:

## Question 43

| Column A | Column B |
|---|---|
| $a > 1$ and $b > 1$, $(2b-1)^a$ where $a, b$ are natural numbers. | $a > 1$ and $b > 1$, $a^{-b-1}$ where $a, b$ are natural numbers. |

Answer:

## Question 44

| Column A | Column B |
|---|---|
| $a > 0$ and $b > 0$, $12\sqrt{2a} + 24\sqrt{5b}$ where $a, b$ are natural numbers. | $a > 0$ and $b > 0$, $12\sqrt{2a + 5b}$ where $a, b$ are natural numbers. |

Answer:

Grades 6 and above  Practice Test 2 Session 2

## Question 45

| Column A | Column B |
|---|---|
| Leo is driving at a steady rate of 80 miles per hour. Find the number of minutes it will take Leo to drive 40 miles. | 30 minutes |

Answer:

## Question 46

| Column A | Column B |
|---|---|
| $\{x,y\}$ represents the remainder when $x$ is divided by $y$, $\{6^7, 3\}$ | $\{x,y\}$ represents the remainder when $x$ is divided by $y$, $\{3^9, 6\}$ |

Answer:

## Question 47

| Column A | Column B |
|---|---|
| $x, y, z,$ and $m$ are positive integers. $x = \frac{2}{5}m$ and $y = \frac{3}{7}m$ and $z = \frac{1}{5}y$ $x$ | $x, y, z,$ and $m$ are positive integers. $x = \frac{2}{5}m$ and $y = \frac{3}{7}m$ and $z = \frac{1}{5}y$ $y$ |

Answer:

## Question 48

| Column A | Column B |
|---|---|
| 7 hours 85 minutes<br>+3 hours 25 minutes | 7 hours 20 minutes<br>−    65 minutes |

Answer:

# Question 49

| Column A | Column B |
|---|---|
| $84.7 \times 10^5$ | $8470,000 \div 10^5$ |

Answer:

# Question 50

| Column A | Column B |
|---|---|
| $7|z-15|$ | $7|15-z|$ |

Answer:

# Question 51

| Column A | Column B |
|---|---|
| The value of $g(x)$ in the equation below, when $x = 2$ $$g(x) = 4x^4$$ | The value of $g(x)$ in the equation below, when $x = 5$ $$g(x) = \frac{7x+20}{7}$$ |

Answer:

# Question 52

| Column A | Column B |
|---|---|
| $a = \frac{49}{55}$ and $b = \frac{42}{35}$, $\frac{a}{b}$ | $a = \frac{49}{55}$ and $b = \frac{42}{35}$, $\frac{b}{a}$ |

Answer:

# Question 53

| Column A | Column B |
|---|---|
| $0.755 + 0.004$ | $0.557 + 0.400$ |

Answer:

## Question 54

| Column A | Column B |
|---|---|
| The line $y = \dfrac{x}{20} + 45$ contains the point $(-8, y)$. The $y$-coordinate for the point | The line $y = \dfrac{x}{5} - 12$ contains the point $(x, -8)$. The $x$-coordinate for the point |

Answer:

## Question 55

| Column A | Column B |
|---|---|
| $\dfrac{14}{24} \times \dfrac{27}{40} \times \dfrac{5}{7}$ | $\dfrac{27}{24} \times \dfrac{14}{7} \times \dfrac{5}{40}$ |

Answer:

# Answer Key

## Verbal

| | | | |
|---|---|---|---|
| 1 | B | 29 | C |
| 2 | C | 30 | A |
| 3 | C | 31 | A |
| 4 | B | 32 | C |
| 5 | B | 33 | B |
| 6 | A | 34 | D |
| 7 | C | 35 | A |
| 8 | C | 36 | C |
| 9 | D | 37 | A |
| 10 | B | 38 | A |
| 11 | B | 39 | D |
| 12 | D | 40 | A |
| 13 | B | 41 | B |
| 14 | B | 42 | C |
| 15 | B | 43 | D |
| 16 | C | 44 | B |
| 17 | C | 45 | A |
| 18 | C | 46 | A |
| 19 | A | 47 | B |
| 20 | C | 48 | B |
| 21 | B | 49 | A |
| 22 | C | 50 | D |
| 23 | A | 51 | B |
| 24 | C | 52 | A |
| 25 | D | 53 | C |
| 26 | C | 54 | D |
| 27 | B | 55 | A |
| 28 | A | | |

## Quantitative

| | | | |
|---|---|---|---|
| 1 | B | 29 | B |
| 2 | A | 30 | A |
| 3 | A | 31 | A |
| 4 | C | 32 | C |
| 5 | B | 33 | A |
| 6 | C | 34 | B |
| 7 | B | 35 | A |
| 8 | A | 36 | A |
| 9 | C | 37 | C |
| 10 | B | 38 | C |
| 11 | A | 39 | A |
| 12 | C | 40 | B |
| 13 | A | 41 | B |
| 14 | C | 42 | C |
| 15 | C | 43 | A |
| 16 | C | 44 | A |
| 17 | B | 45 | C |
| 18 | B | 46 | A |
| 19 | B | 47 | B |
| 20 | C | 48 | A |
| 21 | A | 49 | A |
| 22 | B | 50 | C |
| 23 | C | 51 | A |
| 24 | A | 52 | B |
| 25 | A | 53 | B |
| 26 | B | 54 | A |
| 27 | B | 55 | C |
| 28 | A | | |

# Answers key with Explanation

## Verbal

**1** **Answer:** B

**Explanation:** Chronological means in order of time, while ordinal means in order of place.

**2** **Answer:** C

**Explanation:** Sodden means soaked. Thus, rain makes things sodden. Soot means ash. Thus, soot makes things grimy or dirty.

**3** **Answer:** C

**Explanation:** A cottage is a small dwelling and a mansion is a big one. A pond is a small body of water and a lake is a big one.

**4** **Answer:** B

**Explanation:** Conciliate means to gain by pleasing acts. Thus, someone gentle is likely to conciliate. Retaliate means to make return for a similar attack. Thus, someone vengeful is likely to retaliate.

**5** **Answer:** B

**Explanation:** Satire means exaggeration. Therefore, satire is a synonym of parody which means spoof. Perfidy means disloyal. Therefore, perfidy is a synonym of treachery which means betrayal.

**6** **Answer:** A

**Explanation:** Phonetics deals with language as mnemonics deals with memory.

**7** **Answer:** C

**Explanation:** To wildcat means to look for oil, while to forage means to look for food.

**8** **Answer:** C

**Explanation:** Didactic means moralistic. Thus, a characteristic of a teacher is to be didactic. Histrionic means dramatic. Thus, a characteristic of an actor is to be histrionic.

**9** **Answer:** D

**Explanation:** A mosaic is composed of individual tiles, while a film is composed of individual frames.

**10** **Answer:** B

**Explanation:** A fret is a metal strip on the neck of a stringed instrument. Thus, a fret is part of a guitar. A valve is a device in a brass instrument that channels air flow. Thus, a valve is part of a trumpet.

**11** **Answer:** B

**Explanation:** Condensation is a result of humidity as erosion is a result of rainfall.

**12** **Answer:** D

**Explanation:** An abacus is a tool used in calculation, while a sextant is a tool used in navigation.

**13** **Answer:** B

**Explanation:** An appendix comes at the end of a book and an epilogue comes at the end of a play.

Grades 6 and above                                                                              Practice Test 2 Session 1

**14**  **Answer: B**

  **Explanation:** Mourning is the act of sorrowing. Thus, a keen is a sound of mourning. Exuberance is the state of being enthusiastic. Thus, a whoop is a sound of exuberance.

**15**  **Answer: B**

  **Explanation:** A raconteur is a person who tells a story. Thus, the function of a raconteur is to narrate. A host is a person who receives or handles guests. Thus, the function of a host is to entertain.

**16**  **Answer: C**

  **Explanation:** A compass is an instrument used to determine direction, while an odometer is an instrument used to measure mileage.

**17**  **Answer: C**

  **Explanation:** A psychologist is a person who specializes in the study of mind and behavior. Therefore, a psychologist treats neurosis. An ophthalmologist is a person who deals with the structure and diseases of the eye. Therefore, an ophthalmologist treats cataract.

**18**  **Answer: C**

  **Explanation:** A ream is a quantity of paper as a skein is a quantity of yarn.

**19**  **Answer: A**

  **Explanation:** Monk is a member of a religious order. Thus, a characteristic of a monk is to be devoted. Rover is a person who spends time traveling. Thus, a characteristic of a rover is to be wanderlust.

**20**  **Answer: C**

  **Explanation:** Horror results in fear, while slapstick results in laughter.

**21**  **Answer: B**

  **Explanation:** To be phobic is to be extremely fearful and to be asinine is to be extremely silly.

**22**  **Answer: C**

  **Explanation:** Feral means wild. Thus, the opposite of feral is tame. Ephemeral means to last for a very short time. Thus, the opposite of ephemeral is immortal.

**23**  **Answer: A**

  **Explanation:** To frown is a sign of displeasure and to fidget is a sign of restlessness.

**24**  **Answer: C**

  **Explanation:** Laceration is a break in the skin, while perforation is a break in a seal.

**25**  **Answer: D**

  **Explanation:** Someone skeptical is prone to doubt, while someone choleric is prone to anger.

**26**  **Answer: C**

  **Explanation:** A characteristic of a satin is to be smooth and a characteristic of a treacle is to be viscous.

**27**  **Answer: B**

  **Explanation:** Ambition is a desire for success, while avarice is a desire for money.

Grades 6 and above                                    Practice Test 2 Session 1

28  **Answer:** A

  **Explanation:** Probity means righteousness and guile means cheating. Therefore, someone noted for probity is not noted for guile. Industry means hard work and laziness means slack. Therefore, someone noted for industry is not noted for laziness.

29  **Answer:** C

  **Explanation:** To badger is to annoy persistently as to quarrel is to dispute actively.

30  **Answer:** A

  **Explanation:** The opposite of display is hide and the opposite of dither is settle.

31  **Answer:** A

  **Explanation:** Manacle means handcuff. Thus, a manacle is a shackle for the hands. Fetter means chain for the feet. Thus, a fetter is a shackle for the feet.

32  **Answer:** C

  **Explanation:** A revolver is a type of gun and a scimitar is a type of saber.

33  **Answer:** B

  **Explanation:** A license is a document acknowledging a marriage, while a receipt is a document acknowledging a purchase.

34  **Answer:** D

  **Explanation:** An obsession is a greater degree of interest, while a fantasy is a greater degree of dream.

35  **Answer:** A

  **Explanation:** A cacophony is an unpleasant sound and a stench is an unpleasant smell.

36  **Answer:** C

  **Explanation:** Imaginative means creative. Thus, a characteristic of an inventor is to be imaginative. Erudite means knowledgeable. Thus, a characteristic of a professor is to be erudite.

37  **Answer:** A

  **Explanation:** Worship and reverence are synonyms meaning to honor or respect. Rage and enthusiasm are synonyms meaning intense feelings.

38  **Answer:** A

  **Explanation:** Partisan is a synonym of biased and finite is a synonym of limited.

39  **Answer:** D

  **Explanation:** A conductor leads an orchestra, while a skipper leads a crew.

40  **Answer:** A

  **Explanation:** Frond is a large leaf. Thus, a palm tree has fronds. Quill is a hollow horny shaft. Thus, a porcupine has quills.

41  **Answer:** B

  **Explanation:** To sneer is to smile. Therefore, sneer is a sign of contempt. To glower is to glare. Therefore, glower is a sign of anger.

42  **Answer:** C

   **Explanation:** Something dappled is covered in spots as something riddled is filled with holes.

43  **Answer:** D

   **Explanation:** To dilate is to increase in size and to proliferate is to increase in number.

44  **Answer:** B

   **Explanation:** An arena is a place where conflict takes place, while a forum is a place where debate takes place.

45  **Answer:** A

   **Explanation:** A sham is another word for hoax meaning fake. A brig is another word for prison meaning a place for confinement of offenders.

46  **Answer:** A

   **Explanation:** The opposite of to praise is to insult, while the opposite of to mumble is to enunciate.

47  **Answer:** B

   **Explanation:** Baste is a cooking term which means to moisten food with butter, while mulch is a gardening term which is a protective covering on the ground.

48  **Answer:** B

   **Explanation:** To reprove and to chide are synonyms meaning to scold. To approve and to sanction are synonyms meaning to ratify.

49  **Answer:** A

   **Explanation:** Someone who is hungry is very ravenous, while someone who is heavy is very leaden.

50  **Answer:** D

   **Explanation:** Garner means earn and garble means distort.

51  **Answer:** B

   **Explanation:** Limp means to walk lamely. Thus, a limp is a result of injury. Incarceration means to confine in a jail. Thus, incarceration is a result of conviction.

52  **Answer:** A

   **Explanation:** A sectarian supports a particular sect as a partisan supports a particular cause.

53  **Answer:** C

   **Explanation:** A dirge is a song used at a funeral, while a jingle is a song used in a commercial.

54  **Answer:** D

   **Explanation:** To petrify is to turn to stone, while to ossify is to turn to bone.

55  **Answer:** A

   **Explanation:** A placental is a type of mammal as a melodrama is a type of drama.

**Grades 6 and above**            **Practice Test 2 Session 2**

# Quantitative

**1**   **Answer:** B

**Explanation:** Column A is $2 + 6^2 - 5 - 9 = 2 + 36 - 14 = 24$ whereas column B is $(2+6)^2 - 5 - 9 = 64 - 14 = 50$. Therefore, column B is greater. The correct answer is (B).

**2**   **Answer:** A

**Explanation:** Assume $y = 2$, Column A is $9\sqrt{2} = 12.72$ whereas column B is $\sqrt{9(2)} = \sqrt{18} = 4.24$. Therefore, column A is greater. The correct answer is (A).

**3**   **Answer:** A

**Explanation:** Column A is $\frac{3}{4}z = 0.75z$ whereas column B is $\frac{54}{100}z = 0.54z$. Therefore, column A is greater. The correct answer is (A).

**4**   **Answer:** C

**Explanation:** Column A is,

$$\frac{1}{5}y + \frac{1}{5}y + \frac{1}{5}y + \frac{1}{5}y + \frac{1}{5}y = 20$$
$$\frac{1+1+1+1+1}{5}y = 20$$
$$\frac{5}{5}y = 20$$
$$y = 20$$

whereas column B is also 20. Therefore, both columns are equal. The correct answer is (C).

**5**   **Answer:** B

**Explanation:** Assume $a = 5$ and $b = 5$, Column A is $(5-1)^5 = 4^5 = 1,024$ whereas column B is $(5)^{(5)} = 3,125$. Therefore, column B is greater. The correct answer is (B).

**6**   **Answer:** C

**Explanation:** As it is known that February month may be 28 or 29 days. Therefore, both columns are equal. The correct answer is (C).

**7**   **Answer:** B

**Explanation:** Assume $x = 5$ and $y = 5$, Column A is $\frac{x^2}{x^2 + y} = \frac{5^2}{5^2 + 5} = \frac{5}{5+1} = \frac{5}{6}$ whereas column B is $\frac{x^2}{x^2 - y} = \frac{5^2}{5^2 - 5} = \frac{5}{5-1} = \frac{5}{4}$. Therefore, column B is greater. The correct answer is (B).

**8**   **Answer:** A

**Explanation:** Column A is $5 + \frac{15}{60} = \frac{300+15}{60} = \frac{315}{60} = 5.25$ whereas column B is $\frac{12}{100} - \frac{7}{500} = \frac{60-7}{500} = \frac{53}{500} = 0.106$. Therefore, column A is greater. The correct answer is (A).

**9**   **Answer:** C

**Explanation:** Column A is $\left(b^7\right)^4 = b^{7 \cdot 4} = b^{28}$ whereas column B is $b^7 b^7 b^7 b^7 = b^{7+7+7+7} = b^{28}$. Therefore, both columns are equal. The correct answer is (C).

Grades 6 and above | Practice Test 2 Session 2

**10** Answer: B

Explanation: Column A is $f(6) = -10(6)^3 = -10(216) = -2160$ whereas column B is $f(40) = -\dfrac{40-4}{5} = -8.8$.

Therefore, column B is greater. The correct answer is (B).

**11** Answer: A

Explanation: Column A is $0.353$ whereas column B is $0.335$. Therefore, column A is greater. The correct answer is (A).

**12** Answer: C

Explanation: The absolute value of column A is 99 whereas column B is also 99. Therefore, both columns are equal. The correct answer is (C).

**13** Answer: A

Explanation: Column A is $3k \cdot 1 = 18 \Rightarrow k = 6$ whereas column B is $3k + 1 = 18 \Rightarrow 3k = 17 \Rightarrow k = 5.66$. Therefore, column A is greater. The correct answer is (A).

**14** Answer: C

Explanation: Column A is 1 as $1 \times 9 = 9$ whereas column B is 1 as $1 \times 7 = 7$. Therefore, both columns are equal. The correct answer is (C).

**15** Answer: C

Explanation: Column A is $35 \times 30$ whereas column B is $(35 \times 15) + (35 \times 15) = 35 \times (15 + 15) = 35 \times 30$. Therefore, both columns are equal. The correct answer is (C).

**16** Answer: C

Explanation: Column A is $-23 + (-6) = -23 - 6 = -29$ whereas column B is $-23 - 6 = -29$. Therefore, both columns are equal. The correct answer is (C).

**17** Answer: B

Explanation: Column A can be 0, 1, 2, 3, 4, 5, 6, 7, 8 whereas column B is 9. Therefore, column B is greater. The correct answer is (B).

**18** Answer: B

Explanation: Column A is $5^4 = 5 \cdot 5 \cdot 5 \cdot 5 = 625$ whereas column B is $10^5 = 10 \cdot 10 \cdot 10 \cdot 10 \cdot 10 = 100,000$. Therefore, column B is greater. The correct answer is (B).

**19** Answer: B

Explanation: Column A is $50 \times 0.01 = 0.5$ whereas column B is $\dfrac{12}{15} = 0.8$. Therefore, column B is greater. The correct answer is (B).

**20** Answer: C

Explanation: Column A is $\dfrac{2}{9} \times \dfrac{5}{7} \times \dfrac{3}{6} = \dfrac{5}{63} = 0.079$ whereas column B is $\dfrac{3}{7} \times \dfrac{2}{6} \times \dfrac{5}{9} = \dfrac{5}{63} = 0.079$. Therefore, both columns are equal. The correct answer is (C).

**21** Answer: A

Explanation: Column A is $y = -3(-4) - 10 = 2$ whereas column B is $-4 = -3x - 10 \Rightarrow -3x = 6 \Rightarrow x = -2$. Therefore, column A is greater. The correct answer is (A).

**Grades 6 and above**                                            **Practice Test 2 Session 2**

---

**22**   Answer: B

Explanation: Assume $a = 1$ and $b = -1$, Column A is $\sqrt{5} - \sqrt{6} = 2.236 - 2.449 = -0.213$ whereas column B is $\sqrt{5+6} = \sqrt{11} = 3.316$. Therefore, column B is greater. The correct answer is (B).

**23**   Answer: C

Explanation: The time taken by Essa to drive 25 miles is 30 minutes as Essa is driving 50 miles in 60 minutes. Therefore, both columns are equal. The correct answer is (C).

**24**   Answer: A

Explanation: Column A is $\dfrac{10^4}{40} = \dfrac{10,000}{40} = 250$ whereas column B is $\dfrac{40^2}{10} = \dfrac{1600}{10} = 160$. Therefore, column A is greater. The correct answer is (A).

**25**   Answer: A

Explanation: Assume $m = 2$, Column A is $y = \dfrac{5}{4}(2) = 2.5$ whereas column B is $z = \dfrac{7}{10}(2.5) = 1.75$. Therefore, column A is greater. The correct answer is (A).

**26**   Answer: B

Explanation: Column A is 61 whereas column B is 63. Therefore, column B is greater. The correct answer is (B).

**27**   Answer: B

Explanation: Column A is $\sqrt{\dfrac{43}{20}} = 1.466$ whereas column B is $\sqrt{\dfrac{43}{\sqrt{40}}} = \sqrt{\dfrac{43}{6.324}} = 2.607$. Therefore, column B is greater. The correct answer is (B).

**28**   Answer: A

Explanation: As it is known that $1000\text{m} = 1\text{ kilometer}$. Column A is 500 meters whereas column B is 100 meters as $\dfrac{50}{500} \times 1000 = 100$. Therefore, column A is greater. The correct answer is (A).

**29**   Answer: B

Explanation: Assume $k = -2$, Column A is $45k = 45(-2) = -90$ whereas column B is $k^3 = (-2)^3 = -8$.

Therefore, column B is greater. The correct answer is (B).

**30**   Answer: A

Explanation: As it is known that 1 hour is equal to 60 minutes. Column A is,

       6 hours 35 minutes
     +2 hours 25 minutes
       8 hours 60 minutes

whereas column B is,

       5 hours 40 minutes
   −          25 minutes .
       5 hours 15 minutes

Therefore, column A is greater. The correct answer is (A).

| Grades 6 and above | Practice Test 2 Session 2 |

**31** **Answer:** A

**Explanation:** Column A is $93.5 \times 10^4 = 935 \times 10^4 \times 10^{-1} = 935,000$ whereas column B is $92,100,000 \div 10^4 = \dfrac{92 \times 10^5}{10^4} = 920$. Therefore, column A is greater. The correct answer is (A).

**32** **Answer:** C

**Explanation:** The absolute value of column A is $|z - 15| = z - 15$ whereas column B is $|15 - z| = |(-1)(z - 15)| = z - 15$. Therefore, both columns are equal. The correct answer is (C).

**33** **Answer:** A

**Explanation:** Column A is $\dfrac{2}{3}(72) = 2 \cdot 24 = 48$ whereas column B is 47. Therefore, column A is greater. The correct answer is (A).

**34** **Answer:** B

**Explanation:** Column A is $\dfrac{12/23}{23/12} = \dfrac{12 \cdot 12}{23 \cdot 23} = \dfrac{144}{529} = 0.2722$ whereas column B is $\dfrac{529}{144} = 3.6736$ Therefore, column B is greater. The correct answer is (B).

**35** **Answer:** A

**Explanation:** Column A is some positive number whereas column B is some negative number as even power gives positive quantity and odd power gives negative quantity. Therefore, column A is greater. The correct answer is (A).

**36** **Answer:** A

**Explanation:** Column A is $\left(a^5\right)^4 = a^{5 \cdot 4} = a^{20}$ whereas column B is $\sqrt{a^{19}} = a^{19/2} = a^{9.5}$. Therefore, column A is greater. The correct answer is (A).

**37** **Answer:** C

**Explanation:** Column A is $(-1)0(1)(2)(3)(4) = 0$ whereas column B is $(-3)(-2)(-1)0(1)(2)(3)(4)(5) = 0$. Therefore, both columns are equal. The correct answer is (C).

**38** **Answer:** C

**Explanation:** Column A is $\dfrac{9x + 63}{9} = \dfrac{9(x + 7)}{9} = x + 7$ which is equal to column B. Therefore, both columns are equal. The correct answer is (C).

**39** **Answer:** A

**Explanation:** Column A is greater than column B. The correct answer is (A).

**40** **Answer:** B

**Explanation:** Column A is $12 + 4^2 - 8 - 7 = 12 + 16 - 15 = 13$ whereas column B is $(12 + 4)^2 - 8 - 7 = 196 - 15 = 181$. Therefore, column B is greater. The correct answer is (B).

**41** **Answer:** B

**Explanation:** Assume $x = 3$, Column A is $-42\sqrt{3} = -72.74$ whereas column B is $\sqrt{12 \cdot 3} = \sqrt{36} = 6$. Therefore, column B is greater. The correct answer is (B).

**Grades 6 and above**                                                                    **Practice Test 2 Session 2**

42   **Answer:** C

      **Explanation:** Column A is,

$$\frac{1}{6}z + \frac{1}{6}z + \frac{1}{6}z + \frac{1}{6}z + \frac{1}{6}z + \frac{1}{6}z = 24$$
$$\frac{1+1+1+1+1+1}{6}z = 24$$
$$\frac{6}{6}z = 24$$
$$z = 24$$

      whereas column B is also 24. Therefore, both columns are equal. The correct answer is (C).

43   **Answer:** A

      **Explanation:** Assume $a = 2$ and $b = 2$, Column A is $(2(2)-1)^2 = 3^2 = 9$ whereas column B is $2^{-2-1} = \frac{1}{8} = 0.125$. Therefore, column A is greater. The correct answer is (A).

44   **Answer:** A

      **Explanation:** Assume $a = 3$ and $b = 3$, Column A is $12\sqrt{2(3)} + 24\sqrt{5(3)} = 12\sqrt{6} + 24\sqrt{15} = 29.39 + 92.95 = 122.34$ whereas column B is $12\sqrt{2(3)+5(3)} = 12\sqrt{6+15} = 12\sqrt{21} = 54.99$. Therefore, column A is greater. The correct answer is (A).

45   **Answer:** C

      **Explanation:** The time taken by Leo to drive 40 miles is 30 minutes as Leo is driving 80 miles in 60 minutes. Therefore, both columns are equal. The correct answer is (C).

46   **Answer:** A

      **Explanation:** Column A is $\frac{6^7}{3} = \frac{279,936}{3} = 93,312$ whereas column B is $\frac{3^9}{6} = \frac{19,683}{6} = 3,280.5$. Therefore, column A is greater. The correct answer is (A).

47   **Answer:** B

      **Explanation:** Assume $m = 4$, Column A is $x = \frac{2}{5}(4) = 1.6$ whereas column B is $y = \frac{3}{7}(4) = 1.714$. Therefore, column B is greater. The correct answer is (B).

48   **Answer:** A

      **Explanation:** As it is known that 1 hour is equal to 60 minutes. Column A is,

```
  8 hours 25 minutes
 +3 hours 25 minutes
 11 hours 50 minutes
```

      whereas column B is,

```
  7 hours 20 minutes
 -1 hours 05 minutes .
  6 hours 15 minutes
```

      Therefore, column A is greater. The correct answer is (A).

**Grades 6 and above**  Practice Test 2 Session 2

**49** Answer: A

Explanation: Column A is $84.7 \times 10^5 = 847 \times 10^{-1} \times 10^5 = 8,470,000$ whereas column B is $8470,000 \div 10^5 = \dfrac{847 \times 10^4}{10^5} = 84.7$. Therefore, column A is greater. The correct answer is (A).

**50** Answer: C

Explanation: The absolute value of column A is $7|z-15| = 7(z-15)$ whereas column B is $7|15-z| = 7|(-1)(z-15)| = 7(z-15)$. Therefore, both columns are equal. The correct answer is (C).

**51** Answer: A

Explanation: Column A is $g(2) = 4(2)^4 = 64$ whereas column B is $g(5) = \dfrac{7(5)+20}{7} = \dfrac{55}{7} = 7.8571$. Therefore, column A is greater. The correct answer is (A).

**52** Answer: B

Explanation: Column A is $\dfrac{49/55}{42/35} = \dfrac{49 \cdot 35}{42 \cdot 55} = \dfrac{1715}{2310} = 0.7424$ whereas column B is $\dfrac{2310}{1715} = 1.3469$. Therefore, column B is greater. The correct answer is (B).

**53** Answer: B

Explanation: Column A is $0.759$ whereas column B is $0.957$. Therefore, column B is greater. The correct answer is (B).

**54** Answer: A

Explanation: Column A is $y = \dfrac{(-8)}{20} + 45 = 44.6$ whereas column B is $(-8) = \dfrac{x}{5} - 12 \Rightarrow 4 = \dfrac{x}{5} \Rightarrow x = 20$. Therefore, column A is greater. The correct answer is (A).

**55** Answer: C

Explanation: Column A is $\dfrac{14}{24} \times \dfrac{27}{40} \times \dfrac{5}{7} = \dfrac{135}{480} = 0.28125$ whereas column B is $\dfrac{27}{24} \times \dfrac{14}{7} \times \dfrac{5}{40} = \dfrac{135}{480} = 0.28125$. Therefore, both columns are equal. The correct answer is (C).

# Practice Test 3

# Verbal Practice Test

**Directions:**

Each question begins with two words. These two words go together in a certain way. Under them, there are four other pairs of words lettered A, B, C, and D.

Find the lettered pair of words that go together in the same way as the first pair of words.

1. expand: condense
   - A. endless: eternal
   - B. stale: fresh
   - C. fallacy: illusion
   - D. extinguish: smash

Answer:

2. pilgrims: caravan
   - A. countries: league
   - B. sheep: shoal
   - C. soldiers: crowd
   - D. termites: swarm

Answer:

3. gardener: harrow
   - A. teacher: follow
   - B. engineer: site
   - C. blacksmith: anvil
   - D. plumber: lumber

Answer:

Grades 6 and above                                     Practice Test 3 Session 1

**4**  paleontology: soil

　　A. ornithology: omnivore

　　B. craniology: skull

　　C. cardiology: exercise

　　D. entomology: animal

Answer:

**5**  cock: strut

　　A. lion: prowl

　　B. cattle: herd

　　C. sparrow: chirp

　　D. lamb: gallop

Answer:

**6**  cup: crockery

　　A. phone: battery

　　B. apron: pottery

　　C. curtain: drapery

　　D. book: cookery

Answer:

**7**  clothes: wardrobe

　　A. medicines: dispensary

　　B. sweater: garment

　　C. bees: aviary

　　D. wine: granary

Answer:

**8**  bachelor: spinster

　　A. teacher: student

　　B. queen: prince

　　C. colt: filly

　　D. convict: prisoner

Answer:

**Grades 6 and above**  Practice Test 3 Session 1

**9** paper: origami

A. osier: basketry

B. glass: weapon

C. plastic: masonry

D. picture: frame

Answer:

**10** fireplace: house

A. smoke: cigarette

B. trellis: garden

C. limestone: forest

D. treasure: ocean

Answer:

**11** deficient: complete

A. sufficient: enough

B. magnificent: splendid

C. kinetic: static

D. fragmental: incomplete

Answer:

**12** fuzzy: clarity

A. apparent: clear

B. failure: scarcity

C. buzzy: noisy

D. rigid: flexibility

Answer:

**13** theology: religion

A. biology: human

B. phenology: climate

C. anthropology: artifact

D. seismology: disease

Answer:

Grades 6 and above                                    Practice Test 3 Session 1

**14** foyer: house

   A. vestibule: building

   B. window: room

   C. messenger: office

   D. player: arena

Answer:

**15** snarl: mess

   A. spool: spindle

   B. sputter: drool

   C. pitch: spiel

   D. knot: disentangle

Answer:

**16** solve: mystery

   A. decipher: code

   B. encrypt: clue

   C. recite: answer

   D. conquer: competition

Answer:

**17** expel: pupil

   A. educate: teacher

   B. propel: driver

   C. deport: alien

   D. gargle: person

Answer:

**18** malinger: work

   A. fulfill: ambition

   B. fight: enemy

   C. shirk: obligation

   D. purchase: money

Answer:

Grades 6 and above                                    Practice Test 3 Session 1

**19** patron: support

  A. muse: inspiration

  B. parent: attention

  C. braggart: care

  D. soldier: fight

Answer:

**20** curator: museum

  A. conductor: canteen

  B. warden: prison

  C. servant: restaurant

  D. athlete: sport

Answer:

**21** epic: poem

  A. anecdote: narrative

  B. anthem: hymn

  C. symphony: music

  D. band: opera

Answer:

**22** synthesis: parts

  A. confluence: streams

  B. analogous: parallels

  C. emulsion: milk

  D. fission: elements

Answer:

**23** equity: fairness

  A. impious: reverent

  B. esteem: disgrace

  C. shame: ignominy

  D. equality: imparity

Answer:

86

Grades 6 and above  Practice Test 3 Session 1

**24** examine: scrutinize

    A. pulsate: throb

    B. ratify: decline

    C. challenge: conquer

    D. essential: dispensable

Answer:

**25** replicate: copy

    A. duplicate: original

    B. intricate: simple

    C. allocate: task

    D. supplicate: beg

Answer:

**26** plucky: courageous

    A. indignant: delighted

    B. lucky: hapless

    C. slack: negligent

    D. valiant: coward

Answer:

**27** plume: feather

    A. artery: blood

    B. dump: house

    C. flume: gorge

    D. caliber: bullet

Answer:

**28** unusual: novelty

    A. familiar: standard

    B. mural: painting

    C. deficit: poverty

    D. peculiar: typical

Answer:

**Grades 6 and above**  Practice Test 3 Session 1

**29** incumbent: office

    **A.** fire: station

    **B.** president: country

    **C.** monarch: throne

    **D.** group: accommodation

Answer:

**30** neophyte: experience

    **A.** protestor: protest

    **B.** captain: magnate

    **C.** vagrant: abode

    **D.** veteran: expert

Answer:

**31** pass: mountain

    **A.** route: avenue

    **B.** climb: wall

    **C.** ford: stream

    **D.** elevator: building

Answer:

**32** Siamese: cat

    **A.** type: breed

    **B.** collar: leash

    **C.** sandals: shoes

    **D.** romaine: lettuce

Answer:

**33** division: section

    **A.** layer: tier

    **B.** chapter: verse

    **C.** tether: bundle

    **D.** multiplication: group

Answer:

Grades 6 and above                                            Practice Test 3 Session 1

**34**  optical: sight

   A. digestion: taste

   B. olfactory: smell

   C. rough: touch

   D. earlobe: hear

Answer:

**35**  malice: charity

   A. translucence: transparency

   B. retreat: materialize

   C. decent: immoral

   D. glee: gloom

Answer:

**36**  cask: wine

   A. spoon: fork

   B. pedal: bicycle

   C. valise: clothing

   D. wealth: money

Answer:

**37**  portion: food

   A. dose: drug

   B. slice: muffin

   C. amount: day

   D. pinch: pizza

Answer:

**38**  covert: action

   A. cerebral: think

   B. evanescent: vanish

   C. furtive: behavior

   D. shelter: place

Answer:

89

**Grades 6 and above**  Practice Test 3 Session 1

**39** gag: speech

　A. babble: language

　B. giggle: laugh

　C. fetter: movement

　D. catacomb: vault

Answer:

**40** beacon: light

　A. shroud: garment

　B. precept: principle

　C. instruction: direction

　D. diamond: bright

Answer:

**41** rainbow: downpour

　A. January: February

　B. future: forecast

　C. sunshine: sunrise

　D. postmortem: death

Answer:

**42** pallid: color

　A. tactless: diplomacy

　B. tasteless: food

　C. shade: hue

　D. fade: wither

Answer:

**43** spatula: lifting

　A. bowl: frying

　B. sponge: whitening

　C. scalpel: incising

　D. mask: sleeping

Answer:

Grades 6 and above

Practice Test 3 Session 1

**44** seaworthy: sailing

    A. portable: watching

    B. potable: drinking

    C. worthy: deserving

    D. lucky: ill-fated

Answer:

**45** bonsai: pot

    A. hibiscus: herb

    B. sequoia: forest

    C. wheat: vase

    D. pine: house

Answer:

**46** baton: orchestra

    A. wand: magician

    B. stick: twig

    C. pylon: traffic

    D. mouse: computer

Answer:

**47** pine: coniferous

    A. fern: poisonous

    B. moss: algae

    C. oak: deciduous

    D. acacia: herbaceous

Answer:

**48** barrack: base

    A. adobe: desert

    B. tank: field

    C. storm: typhoon

    D. lodge: quarter

Answer:

Grades 6 and above

Practice Test 3 Session 1

**49** specific: generic
   A. particular: detail
   B. fatuous: sensible
   C. annoy: irritate
   D. industrious: diligent

Answer:

**50** embassy: ambassador
   A. office: executive
   B. cage: bird
   C. country: president
   D. forest: eagle

Answer:

**51** historian: past
   A. teller: fortune
   B. seer: future
   C. cashier: register
   D. reporter: weather

Answer:

**52** grim: somber
   A. prim: neat
   B. timid: venturous
   C. trim: spoil
   D. grin: frown

Answer:

**53** cacophony: noise
   A. symphony: music
   B. drapery: cloth
   C. drudgery: work
   D. lottery: prize

Answer:

**54** disgust: emotion

    A. message: letter

    B. bush: shrub

    C. folktale: literature

    D. shark: reptile

Answer:

**55** stumble: fall

    A. thimble: sew

    B. gamble: money

    C. dribble: roll

    D. truckle: bow

Answer:

# Optional Break

# Quantitative Practice Test

### Directions:

Each question given below has two parts. One part is column A, the other part is column B. You must find out if one part is greater than the other, or if the parts are equal, you will choose one answer.

A. If the part in column A is greater

B. If the part in column B is greater

C. The two parts are equal

D. If the relationship cannot be determined from the information given.

**Question 1**

| Column A | Column B |
|---|---|
| The line $y = 5x + 24$ contains the point $(-5, y)$.<br>The $y$-coordinate for the point | The line $y = -3x + 14$ contains the point $(x, -5)$.<br>The $x$-coordinate for the point |

Answer:

**Question 2**

| Column A | Column B |
|---|---|
| $a > 0$ and $b > 0$, $\sqrt{7a} - \sqrt{4b^2}$ where $a$, $b$ are natural numbers. | $a > 0$ and $b > 0$, $\sqrt{7a + 4b^2}$ where $a$, $b$ are natural numbers. |

Answer:

**Grades 6 and above**                                                 **Practice Test 3 Session 2**

## Question 3

| Column A | Column B |
| --- | --- |
| Evelyn is driving at a steady rate of 120 miles per hour. Find the number of minutes it will take Evelyn to drive 60 miles. | 30 minutes |

Answer:

## Question 4

| Column A | Column B |
| --- | --- |
| $\{x,y\}$ represents the remainder when $x$ is divided by $y$, $\{9^4, 6\}$ | $\{x,y\}$ represents the remainder when $x$ is divided by $y$, $\{6^9, 4\}$ |

Answer:

## Question 5

| Column A | Column B |
| --- | --- |
| $x, y, z,$ and $m$ are positive integers. $x = -\frac{8}{3}m$ and $y = \frac{2}{6}m$ and $z = \frac{10}{9}y$ <br><br> $y$ | $x, y, z,$ and $m$ are positive integers. $x = -\frac{8}{3}m$ and $y = \frac{2}{6}m$ and $z = \frac{10}{9}y$ <br><br> $x$ |

Answer:

## Question 6

| Column A | Column B |
| --- | --- |
| The greatest odd number less than 95 | The least odd number greater than 93 |

Answer:

Grades 6 and above                                              Practice Test 3 Session 2

## Question 7

| Column A | Column B |
|----------|----------|
| $\sqrt{\dfrac{74}{35}}$ | $\sqrt{\dfrac{74}{\sqrt{35}}}$ |

Answer:

## Question 8

| Column A | Column B |
|----------|----------|
| A distance of 200 meters | A distance of $\dfrac{50}{200}$ kilometers |

Answer:

## Question 9

| Column A | Column B |
|----------|----------|
| $k < 0$, $-9k$ where $k$ is an integer. | $k < 0$, $-7k$ where $k$ is an integer. |

Answer:

## Question 10

| Column A | Column B |
|----------|----------|
| 4 hours 25 minutes<br>+1 hours 15 minutes | 7 hours 50 minutes<br>−        05 minutes |

Answer:

## Question 11

| Column A | Column B |
|----------|----------|
| $7.56 \times 10^3$ | $75{,}600{,}000 \div 10^5$ |

Answer:

# Grades 6 and above  Practice Test 3 Session 2

## Question 12

| Column A | Column B |
|---|---|
| $\lvert x - 85 \rvert$ | $\lvert 85 - x \rvert$ |

Answer:

## Question 13

| Column A | Column B |
|---|---|
| A class used 81 packages of cheese to make pizzas. Each pizza used $\frac{2}{3}$ a package of cheese. Find the number of pizzas they made. | 53 |

Answer:

## Question 14

| Column A | Column B |
|---|---|
| $a = \frac{25}{54}$ and $b = \frac{55}{24}$, $\frac{a}{b}$ | $a = \frac{12}{23}$ and $b = \frac{23}{12}$, $\frac{b}{a}$ |

Answer:

## Question 15

| Column A | Column B |
|---|---|
| $(-45)^8$ | $(-101)^{13}$ |

Answer:

## Question 16

| Column A | Column B |
|---|---|
| $(a^{-9})^3$ where $a$ is a natural number. | $\sqrt{a^{24}}$ where $a$ is a natural number. |

Answer:

Grades 6 and above  Practice Test 3 Session 2

## Question 17

| Column A | Column B |
|---|---|
| The product of the integers from −4 to 1. | The product of the integers from 0 to 6. |

Answer:

## Question 18

| Column A | Column B |
|---|---|
| $\dfrac{5x+75}{5}$ | $x+15$ |

Answer:

## Question 19

| Column A | Column B |
|---|---|
| .79 | .079 |

Answer:

## Question 20

| Column A | Column B |
|---|---|
| $4+7^2-9-1$ | $(4+7)^2-9-1$ |

Answer:

## Question 21

| Column A | Column B |
|---|---|
| $7+3^2-8-4$ | $(7+3)^2-8-4$ |

Answer:

**Grades 6 and above**  Practice Test 3 Session 2

## Question 22

| Column A | Column B |
|---|---|
| $y > 1$, $12\sqrt{y}$ where $y$ is a natural number. | $y > 1$, $\sqrt{12y}$ where $y$ is a natural number. |

Answer:

## Question 23

| Column A | Column B |
|---|---|
| $\frac{5}{20}$ of $z$ | 30% of $z$ |

Answer:

## Question 24

| Column A | Column B |
|---|---|
| $\frac{1}{3}y + \frac{1}{3}y + \frac{1}{3}y = 10$, $y$ | $\frac{1}{3}y + \frac{1}{3}y + \frac{1}{3}y = 10$, 10 |

Answer:

## Question 25

| Column A | Column B |
|---|---|
| $a > 1$ and $b > 1$, $(a^2 + 2)^{(b-1)}$ where $a, b$ are natural numbers. | $a > 1$ and $b > 1$, $a^{b^2}$ where $a, b$ are natural numbers. |

Answer:

## Question 26

| Column A | Column B |
|---|---|
| 29 days | February month |

Answer:

Grades 6 and above     Practice Test 3 Session 2

## Question 27

| Column A | Column B |
|---|---|
| $x > y > 0$, $-\dfrac{x^{2x}}{xy^{2y}}$ where $x, y$ are natural numbers. | $x > y > 0$, $\dfrac{x^{2x}}{xy^{2y}}$ where $x, y$ are natural numbers. |

Answer:

## Question 28

| Column A | Column B |
|---|---|
| $25 + \dfrac{0.5}{10}$ | $\dfrac{1.22}{500} - \dfrac{8}{1000}$ |

Answer:

## Question 29

| Column A | Column B |
|---|---|
| $\left(b^{-2}\right)^3$ | $b^{-2}b^{-2}b^{-2}$ |

Answer:

## Question 30

| Column A | Column B |
|---|---|
| The value of $a(x)$ in the equation below, when $x = 9$ $$a(x) = -9x^2$$ | The value of $a(x)$ in the equation below, when $x = 7$ $$a(x) = -\dfrac{9x+7}{2}$$ |

Answer:

Grades 6 and above   Practice Test 3 Session 2

## Question 31

| Column A | Column B |
|---|---|
| $0.454 + 0.003$ | $0.545 + 0.300$ |

Answer:

## Question 32

| Column A | Column B |
|---|---|
| $|-454|$ | $|454|$ |

Answer:

## Question 33

| Column A | Column B |
|---|---|
| The value of $k$ if $7k \cdot 1 = 28$ | The value of $k$ if $7k + 1 = 28$ |

Answer:

## Question 34

| Column A | Column B |
|---|---|
| The value of a number if 19 times the number is 19. | The value of a number if 71 times the number is 71. |

Answer:

## Question 35

| Column A | Column B |
|---|---|
| $75 \times 40$ | $(75 \times 15) + (75 \times 25)$ |

Answer:

Grades 6 and above  Practice Test 3 Session 2

## Question 36

| Column A | Column B |
|---|---|
| $-487 + (-46)$ | $-487 - 46$ |

Answer:

## Question 37

| Column A | Column B |
|---|---|
| $x < 90$ | 90 |
| $x$ | |

Answer:

## Question 38

| Column A | Column B |
|---|---|
| $8^5$ | $5^8$ |

Answer:

## Question 39

| Column A | Column B |
|---|---|
| $45\%$ | $\dfrac{35}{40}$ |

Answer:

## Question 40

| Column A | Column B |
|---|---|
| $\dfrac{14}{8} \times \dfrac{2}{9} \times \dfrac{23}{7}$ | $\dfrac{23}{9} \times \dfrac{14}{7} \times \dfrac{2}{8}$ |

Answer:

**Grades 6 and above**            Practice Test 3 Session 2

## Question 41

| Column A | Column B |
|---|---|
| $x > 0$, $91\sqrt{x}$ where $x$ is a natural number. | $x > 0$, $\sqrt{24x}$ where $x$ is a natural number. |

Answer:

## Question 42

| Column A | Column B |
|---|---|
| $\frac{1}{7}z + \frac{1}{7}z + \frac{1}{7}z + \frac{1}{7}z + \frac{1}{7}z + \frac{1}{7}z + \frac{1}{7}z = 28$, $z$ | $\frac{1}{7}z + \frac{1}{7}z + \frac{1}{7}z + \frac{1}{7}z + \frac{1}{7}z + \frac{1}{7}z + \frac{1}{7}z = 28$, $28$ |

Answer:

## Question 43

| Column A | Column B |
|---|---|
| $a > 1$ and $b > 1$, $\left(b^{2a+1}\right)^a$ where $a, b$ are natural numbers. | $a > 1$ and $b > 1$, $(a+b)^{b+a}$ where $a, b$ are natural numbers. |

Answer:

## Question 44

| Column A | Column B |
|---|---|
| $a > 0$ and $b > 0$, $48\sqrt{a} + 96\sqrt{b}$ where $a, b$ are natural numbers. | $a > 0$ and $b > 0$, $48\sqrt{a+b}$ where $a, b$ are natural numbers. |

Answer:

# Grades 6 and above                                                       Practice Test 3 Session 2

## Question 45

| Column A | Column B |
| --- | --- |
| Elly is driving at a steady rate of 125 miles per hour. Find the number of minutes it will take Elly to drive 25 miles. | 12 minutes |

Answer:

## Question 46

| Column A | Column B |
| --- | --- |
| $\{x,y\}$ represents the remainder when $x$ is divided by $y$, $\{8^5, 7\}$ | $\{x,y\}$ represents the remainder when $x$ is divided by $y$, $\{7^5, 8\}$ |

Answer:

## Question 47

| Column A | Column B |
| --- | --- |
| $x, y, z,$ and $m$ are positive integers. $x = \dfrac{22}{15}m$ and $y = \dfrac{43}{17}m$ and $z = \dfrac{31}{25}y$ <br><br> $x$ | $x, y, z,$ and $m$ are positive integers. $x = \dfrac{22}{15}m$ and $y = \dfrac{43}{17}m$ and $z = \dfrac{31}{25}y$ <br><br> $y$ |

Answer:

## Question 48

| Column A | Column B |
| --- | --- |
| 9 hours 95 minutes <br> +2 hours 35 minutes | 8 hours 25 minutes <br> −      75 minutes |

Answer:

Grades 6 and above  Practice Test 3 Session 2

## Question 49

| Column A | Column B |
|---|---|
| $68.2 \times 10^3$ | $6{,}820{,}000 \div 10^6$ |

Answer:

## Question 50

| Column A | Column B |
|---|---|
| $8|z-3|$ | $8|3-z|$ |

Answer:

## Question 51

| Column A | Column B |
|---|---|
| The value of $p(x)$ in the equation below, when $x = 5$ $$p(x) = 7x^6$$ | The value of $p(x)$ in the equation below, when $x = 9$ $$p(x) = \frac{9x-39}{9}$$ |

Answer:

## Question 52

| Column A | Column B |
|---|---|
| $a = \dfrac{509}{1045}$ and $b = \dfrac{1078}{524}$, $\dfrac{a}{b}$ | $a = \dfrac{49}{55}$ and $b = \dfrac{42}{35}$, $\dfrac{b}{a}$ |

Answer:

## Question 53

| Column A | Column B |
|---|---|
| $0.975 + 0.003$ | $0.579 + 0.300$ |

Answer:

## Question 54

| Column A | Column B |
|---|---|
| The line $y = -\dfrac{20x}{15} - 89$ contains the point $(-4, y)$. The $y$-coordinate for the point | The line $y = -\dfrac{2x}{15} + 43$ contains the point $(x, -4)$. The $x$-coordinate for the point |

Answer:

## Question 55

| Column A | Column B |
|---|---|
| $\dfrac{48}{14} \times \dfrac{54}{20} \times \dfrac{4}{9}$ | $\dfrac{4}{20} \times \dfrac{48}{9} \times \dfrac{54}{20}$ |

Answer:

# Answer Key

## Verbal

1. B
2. A
3. C
4. B
5. A
6. C
7. A
8. C
9. A
10. B
11. C
12. D
13. B
14. A
15. C
16. A
17. C
18. C
19. A
20. B
21. C
22. A
23. C
24. A
25. D
26. C
27. C
28. A
29. C
30. C
31. C
32. D
33. A
34. B
35. D
36. C
37. A
38. C
39. C
40. B
41. D
42. A
43. C
44. B
45. B
46. C
47. C
48. A
49. B
50. D
51. B
52. A
53. C
54. C
55. D

## Quantitative

1. B
2. B
3. C
4. B
5. A
6. B
7. B
8. B
9. A
10. B
11. A
12. C
13. A
14. B
15. A
16. B
17. C
18. C
19. A
20. B
21. B
22. A
23. B
24. C
25. B
26. C
27. B
28. A
29. C
30. B
31. B
32. C
33. A
34. C
35. C
36. C
37. B
38. B
39. B
40. C
41. A
42. C
43. A
44. A
45. C
46. A
47. B
48. A
49. A
50. C
51. A
52. B
53. A
54. B
55. C

# Answer Key with Explanations

## Verbal

1. **Answer:** B
   **Explanation:** Expand is the opposite of condense as stale is the opposite of fresh.

2. **Answer:** A
   **Explanation:** A group of pilgrims is called caravan as a group of countries is called league.

3. **Answer:** C
   **Explanation:** A harrow is a cultivating tool used by a gardener, while an anvil is a tool on which metal is shaped used by blacksmith.

4. **Answer:** B
   **Explanation:** Paleontology is the study of soil and craniology is the study of skull.

5. **Answer:** A
   **Explanation:** Strut is the name given to the movement of the cock and prowl is the name given to the movement of the lion.

6. **Answer:** C
   **Explanation:** Crockery refers to ceramic tableware. Thus, a cup belongs to the class of crockery. Drapery refers to a decorative piece of material usually hung in loose folds. Thus, a curtain belongs to the class of drapery.

7. **Answer:** A
   **Explanation:** Clothes are kept in a wardrobe as medicines are kept in a dispensary.

8. **Answer:** C
   **Explanation:** Bachelor is an unmarried man, while spinster is an unmarried woman. Colt is a male horse, while filly is a female horse.

9. **Answer:** A
   **Explanation:** Paper is used to make origami as osier is a willow used to make basket.

10. **Answer:** B
    **Explanation:** A fireplace is found in a house, while a trellis is found in a garden.

11. **Answer:** C
    **Explanation:** Deficient means lacking and complete means to be whole. Thus, deficient is the opposite of complete. Kinetic means to be in motion and static means to be at rest. Thus, kinetic is the opposite of static.

12. **Answer:** D
    **Explanation:** Fuzzy means blurry. Therefore, something fuzzy lacks clarity. Rigid means hard. Therefore, something rigid lacks flexibility.

13. **Answer:** B
    **Explanation:** Theology is the study of religion, while phenology is the study of climate.

Grades 6 and above    Practice Test 3 Session 1

**14** Answer: A

Explanation: A foyer is the entrance to a house as a vestibule is the entrance to a building.

**15** Answer: C

Explanation: A snarl is a synonym of mess meaning untidy. A pitch is a synonym of spiel meaning to utter.

**16** Answer: A

Explanation: Mystery is to be solved and code is to be decipher or decode.

**17** Answer: C

Explanation: To expel is to send a pupil away from school, while to deport is to send an alien away from a country.

**18** Answer: C

Explanation: To malinger is to avoid work, while to shirk is to avoid obligation.

**19** Answer: A

Explanation: A patron provides support as a muse provides inspiration.

**20** Answer: B

Explanation: A curator is a person who is in charge of a place of exhibit. Thus, a curator works in a museum. A warden is a person who is in charge of the operation of a prison. Thus, a warden works in a prison.

**21** Answer: C

Explanation: An epic is a long from of poem and a symphony is a long form of music.

**22** Answer: A

Explanation: Synthesis is a combination of parts and a confluence is a combination of streams.

**23** Answer: C

Explanation: Equity is a synonym of fairness meaning free from bias. Shame is a synonym of ignominy meaning disgrace.

**24** Answer: A

Explanation: Examine and scrutinize are synonyms meaning to check or inspect. Pulsate and throb are synonyms meaning to vibrate.

**25** Answer: D

Explanation: To replicate means to copy, while to supplicate means to beg.

**26** Answer: C

Explanation: Someone plucky is courageous, while someone slack is negligent.

**27** Answer: C

Explanation: A flume is a feather and a flume is a gorge.

**28** Answer: A

Explanation: Unusual describes a novelty as familiar describes a standard.

29  **Answer:** C

   **Explanation:** An incumbent occupies an office, while a monarch occupies a throne.

30  **Answer:** C

   **Explanation:** Neophyte is a beginner. Thus, someone neophyte lacks experience. Vagrant is a wanderer with no place to live. Thus, someone vagrant lacks an abode or home.

31  **Answer:** C

   **Explanation:** A pass is a place to cross a mountain as a ford is a place to cross a stream.

32  **Answer:** D

   **Explanation:** Siamese is a kind of cat and a romaine is a kind of lettuce.

33  **Answer:** A

   **Explanation:** Division and section are synonyms and layer and tier are synonyms.

34  **Answer:** B

   **Explanation:** Optical relates to the sense of sight and olfactory relates to the sense of smell.

35  **Answer:** D

   **Explanation:** Malice is a desire to cause injury and charity is a desire to help. Thus, malice is the opposite of charity. Glee means cheerfulness and gloom means frown. Thus, glee is the opposite of gloom.

36  **Answer:** C

   **Explanation:** A cask is a barrel usually for liquids. Therefore, a cask holds wine. A valise is a traveler's case. Therefore, a valise holds clothing.

37  **Answer:** A

   **Explanation:** A portion is a measure of food and a dose is a measure of a drug.

38  **Answer:** C

   **Explanation:** Covert action is secret and stealthy, while furtive behavior is secret and stealthy.

39  **Answer:** C

   **Explanation:** To gag is to restrict use of the mouth. Thus, gag prevents speech. Fetter is a chain for the feet. Thus, fetter prevents movement.

40  **Answer:** B

   **Explanation:** A beacon is a guiding light and a precept is a guiding principle.

41  **Answer:** D

   **Explanation:** A rainbow occurs after a downpour, while a postmortem follows a death.

42  **Answer:** A

   **Explanation:** Pallid means dull. Thus, something pallid lacks in color. Tactless means graceless. Thus, someone tactless lacks diplomacy.

43  **Answer:** C

   **Explanation:** A spatula is used for lifting as scalpel is used for incising.

| | |
|---|---|
| 44 | **Answer:** B |
| | **Explanation:** Something seaworthy is suitable for sailing, while something potable is suitable for drinking. |
| 45 | **Answer:** B |
| | **Explanation:** A bonsai tree is grown in a pot, while a sequoia is grown in forest. |
| 46 | **Answer:** C |
| | **Explanation:** A baton is used to direct an orchestra and a pylon is used to direct a traffic. |
| 47 | **Answer:** C |
| | **Explanation:** Coniferous tree has needle-shaped or scale-like leaves. Therefore, pine is a kind of coniferous tree. Deciduous tree has fall off season. Therefore, oak is a kind of deciduous tree. |
| 48 | **Answer:** A |
| | **Explanation:** A barrack is a structure found on a base and an adobe is a structure found on a desert. |
| 49 | **Answer:** B |
| | **Explanation:** Something specific is not generic and something fatuous is not sensible. |
| 50 | **Answer:** D |
| | **Explanation:** An embassy is the residence of an ambassador and an eagle lives in a forest. |
| 51 | **Answer:** B |
| | **Explanation:** A historian looks in the past as a seer looks in the future. |
| 52 | **Answer:** A |
| | **Explanation:** Grim and somber are synonyms meaning dreary or gloomy. Prim and neat are synonyms meaning clean. |
| 53 | **Answer:** C |
| | **Explanation:** A cacophony is an unpleasant noise as a drudgery is an unpleasant work. |
| 54 | **Answer:** C |
| | **Explanation:** Disgust is a type of emotion and folktale is a type of literature. |
| 55 | **Answer:** D |
| | **Explanation:** To stumble means to fall as to truckle means to bow. |

# Quantitative

1. **Answer:** B

   **Explanation:** Column A is $y = 5(-5) + 24 = -1$ whereas column B is $-5 = -3x + 14 \Rightarrow -3x = -19 \Rightarrow x = 6.333$. Therefore, column B is greater. The correct answer is (B).

2. **Answer:** B

   **Explanation:** Assume $a = 2$ and $b = -1$, Column A is $\sqrt{14} - \sqrt{4} = 3.7416 - 2 = 1.7416$ whereas column B is $\sqrt{14+4} = \sqrt{18} = 4.2426$. Therefore, column B is greater. The correct answer is (B).

Grades 6 and above | Practice Test 3 Session 2

**3** **Answer: C**

**Explanation:** The time taken by Evelyn to drive 60 miles is 30 minutes as Evelyn is driving 120 miles in 60 minutes. Therefore, both columns are equal. The correct answer is (C).

**4** **Answer: B**

**Explanation:** Column A is $\frac{9^4}{6} = \frac{6561}{6} = 1093.5$ whereas column B is $\frac{6^9}{4} = \frac{10,077,696}{4} = 2,519,424$.

Therefore, column B is greater. The correct answer is (B).

**5** **Answer: A**

**Explanation:** Assume $m = 1$, Column A is $y = \frac{2}{6}(1) = 0.33$ whereas column B is $x = -\frac{8}{3}(1) = -2.66$. Therefore, column A is greater. The correct answer is (A).

**6** **Answer: B**

**Explanation:** Column A is 93 whereas column B is 95. Therefore, column B is greater. The correct answer is (B).

**7** **Answer: B**

**Explanation:** Column A is $\sqrt{\frac{74}{35}} = 1.4540$ whereas column B is $\sqrt{\frac{74}{\sqrt{35}}} = \sqrt{\frac{74}{5.916}} = 3.5367$. Therefore, column B is greater. The correct answer is (B).

**8** **Answer: B**

**Explanation:** As it is known that $1000m = 1\text{ kilometer}$. Column A is 200 meters whereas column B is 250 meters as $\frac{50}{200} \times 1000 = 250$. Therefore, column B is greater. The correct answer is (B).

**9** **Answer: A**

**Explanation:** Assume $k = -5$, Column A is $-9k = -9(-5) = 45$ whereas column B is $-7k = -7(-5) = 35$.

Therefore, column A is greater. The correct answer is (A).

**10** **Answer: B**

**Explanation:** As it is known that 1 hour is equal to 60 minutes. Column A is,

```
  4 hours 25 minutes
 +1 hours 15 minutes
  5 hours 40 minutes
```

whereas column B is,

```
  7 hours 50 minutes
 −        05 minutes .
  7 hours 45 minutes
```

Therefore, column B is greater. The correct answer is (B).

**11** **Answer: A**

**Explanation:** Column A is $7.56 \times 10^3 = 756 \times 10^{-2} \times 10^3 = 7560$ whereas column B is $75,600,000 \div 10^5 = \frac{756 \times 10^5}{10^5} = 756$. Therefore, column A is greater. The correct answer is (A).

**12** Answer: C

Explanation: The absolute value of column A is $|x-85| = x-85$ whereas column B is $|85-x| = |(-1)(x-85)| = x-85$. Therefore, both columns are equal. The correct answer is (C).

**13** Answer: A

Explanation: Column A is $\frac{2}{3}(81) = 2 \cdot 27 = 54$ whereas column B is 53. Therefore, column A is greater. The correct answer is (A).

**14** Answer: B

Explanation: Column A is $\frac{25/54}{55/24} = \frac{25 \cdot 24}{55 \cdot 54} = \frac{600}{2970} = 0.2020$ whereas column B is $\frac{2970}{600} = 4.95$ Therefore, column B is greater. The correct answer is (B).

**15** Answer: A

Explanation: Column A is some positive number whereas column B is some negative number as even power gives positive quantity and odd power gives negative quantity. Therefore, column A is greater. The correct answer is (A).

**16** Answer: B

Explanation: Column A is $(a^{-9})^3 = a^{-9 \cdot 3} = a^{-27}$ whereas column B is $\sqrt{a^{24}} = a^{24/2} = a^{12}$. Therefore, column B is greater. The correct answer is (B).

**17** Answer: C

Explanation: Column A is $(-4)(-3)(-2)(-1)0(1) = 0$ whereas column B is $0(1)(2)(3)(4)(5)(6) = 0$. Therefore, both columns are equal. The correct answer is (C).

**18** Answer: C

Explanation: Column A is $\frac{5x+75}{5} = \frac{5(x+15)}{5} = x+15$ which is equal to column B. Therefore, both columns are equal. The correct answer is (C).

**19** Answer: A

Explanation: Column A is greater than column B. The correct answer is (A).

**20** Answer: B

Explanation: Column A is $4 + 7^2 - 9 - 1 = 4 + 49 - 10 = 43$ whereas column B is $(4+7)^2 - 9 - 1 = 121 - 10 = 111$. Therefore, column B is greater. The correct answer is (B).

**21** Answer: B

Explanation: Column A is $7 + 3^2 - 8 - 4 = 7 + 9 - 12 = 4$ whereas column B is $(7+3)^2 - 8 - 4 = 100 - 12 = 88$. Therefore, column B is greater. The correct answer is (B).

**22** Answer: A

Explanation: Assume $y = 3$, Column A is $12\sqrt{3} = 20.784$ whereas column B is $\sqrt{12(3)} = \sqrt{36} = 6$. Therefore, column A is greater. The correct answer is (A).

**23** Answer: B

Explanation: Column A is $\frac{5}{20}z = 0.25z$ whereas column B is $\frac{30}{100}z = 0.30z$. Therefore, column B is greater. The correct answer is (B).

**24** Answer: C

Explanation: Column A is,

$$\frac{1}{3}y + \frac{1}{3}y + \frac{1}{3}y = 10$$
$$\frac{1+1+1}{3}y = 10$$
$$\frac{3}{3}y = 10$$
$$y = 10$$

whereas column B is also 10. Therefore, both columns are equal. The correct answer is (C).

**25** Answer: B

Explanation: Assume $a = 2$ and $b = 2$, Column A is $(2^2 + 2)^{(2-1)} = 6^1 = 6$ whereas column B is $2^{2^2} = 2^4 = 16$. Therefore, column B is greater. The correct answer is (B).

**26** Answer: C

Explanation: As it is known that February month may be 28 or 29 days. Therefore, both columns are equal. The correct answer is (C).

**27** Answer: B

Explanation: Assume $x = 3$ and $y = 3$, Column A is $-\frac{x^{2x}}{xy^{2y}} = -\frac{3^6}{3 \cdot 3^6} = -0.333$ whereas column B is $\frac{x^{2x}}{xy^{2y}} = \frac{3^6}{3 \cdot 3^6} = 0.333$. Therefore, column B is greater. The correct answer is (B).

**28** Answer: A

Explanation: Column A is $25 + \frac{0.5}{10} = \frac{250 + 0.5}{10} = \frac{250.5}{10} = 25.05$ whereas column B is

$\frac{1.22}{500} - \frac{8}{1000} = \frac{2.44 - 8}{1000} = -\frac{5.56}{1000} = -0.00556$. Therefore, column A is greater. The correct answer is (A).

**29** Answer: C

Explanation: Column A is $(b^{-2})^3 = b^{-2 \cdot 3} = b^{-6}$ whereas column B is $b^{-2}b^{-2}b^{-2} = b^{-2-2-2} = b^{-6}$. Therefore, both columns are equal. The correct answer is (C).

**30** Answer: B

Explanation: Column A is $a(9) = -9(9)^2 = -729$ whereas column B is $a(7) = -\frac{9(7)+7}{2} = -35$. Therefore, column B is greater. The correct answer is (B).

**31** Answer: B

Explanation: Column A is $0.457$ whereas column B is $0.845$. Therefore, column B is greater. The correct answer is (B).

32. **Answer:** C

    **Explanation:** The absolute value of column A is 454 whereas column B is also 454. Therefore, both columns are equal. The correct answer is (C).

33. **Answer:** A

    **Explanation:** Column A is $7k \cdot 1 = 28 \Rightarrow k = 4$ whereas column B is $7k + 1 = 28 \Rightarrow 7k = 27 \Rightarrow k = 3.8571$. Therefore, column A is greater. The correct answer is (A).

34. **Answer:** C

    **Explanation:** Column A is 1 as $1 \times 19 = 19$ whereas column B is 1 as $1 \times 71 = 71$. Therefore, both columns are equal. The correct answer is (C).

35. **Answer:** C

    **Explanation:** Column A is $75 \times 40$ whereas column B is $(75 \times 15) + (75 \times 25) = 75 \times (15 + 25) = 75 \times 40$. Therefore, both columns are equal. The correct answer is (C).

36. **Answer:** C

    **Explanation:** Column A is $-487 + (-46) = -487 - 46 = -533$ whereas column B is $-487 - 46 = -533$. Therefore, both columns are equal. The correct answer is (C).

37. **Answer:** B

    **Explanation:** Column A can be 0, 1, 2, 3, 4, 5, 6…., 89 whereas column B is 90. Therefore, column B is greater. The correct answer is (B).

38. **Answer:** B

    **Explanation:** Column A is $8^5 = 8 \cdot 8 \cdot 8 \cdot 8 \cdot 8 = 32,768$ whereas column B is $5^8 = 5 \cdot 5 \cdot 5 \cdot 5 \cdot 5 \cdot 5 \cdot 5 \cdot 5 = 390,625$. Therefore, column B is greater. The correct answer is (B).

39. **Answer:** B

    **Explanation:** Column A is $45 \times 0.01 = 0.45$ whereas column B is $\frac{35}{40} = 0.875$. Therefore, column B is greater. The correct answer is (B).

40. **Answer:** C

    **Explanation:** Column A is $\frac{14}{8} \times \frac{2}{9} \times \frac{23}{7} = \frac{23}{18} = 1.2777$ whereas column B is $\frac{23}{9} \times \frac{14}{7} \times \frac{2}{8} = \frac{23}{18} = 1.2777$.

    Therefore, both columns are equal. The correct answer is (C).

41. **Answer:** A

    **Explanation:** Assume $x = 6$, Column A is $91\sqrt{6} = 222.903$ whereas column B is $\sqrt{24 \cdot 6} = \sqrt{144} = 12$. Therefore, column A is greater. The correct answer is (A).

42. **Answer:** C

    **Explanation:** Column A is,
    $$\frac{1}{7}z + \frac{1}{7}z + \frac{1}{7}z + \frac{1}{7}z + \frac{1}{7}z + \frac{1}{7}z + \frac{1}{7}z = 28$$
    $$\frac{1+1+1+1+1+1+1}{7}z = 28$$
    $$\frac{7}{7}z = 28$$
    $$z = 28$$

    whereas column B is also 28. Therefore, both columns are equal. The correct answer is (C).

Grades 6 and above    Practice Test 3 Session 2

43  **Answer: A**
Explanation: Assume $a = 3$ and $b = 3$, Column A is $\left(3^{2(3)+1}\right)^3 = 3^{21} = 10,460,353,203$ whereas column B is $(3+3)^{3+3} = 6^6 = 46,656$. Therefore, column A is greater. The correct answer is (A).

44  **Answer: A**
Explanation: Assume $a = 1$ and $b = 1$, Column A is $48\sqrt{1} + 96\sqrt{1} = 48 + 96 = 144$ whereas column B is $48\sqrt{1+1} = 48\sqrt{2} = 67.882$. Therefore, column A is greater. The correct answer is (A).

45  **Answer: C**
Explanation: The time taken by Elly to drive 25 miles is 12 minutes as Elly is driving 125 miles in 60 minutes. Therefore, both columns are equal. The correct answer is (C).

46  **Answer: A**
Explanation: Column A is $\dfrac{8^5}{7} = \dfrac{32,768}{7} = 4,681.14$ whereas column B is $\dfrac{7^5}{8} = \dfrac{16,807}{8} = 2,100.87$. Therefore, column A is greater. The correct answer is (A).

47  **Answer: B**
Explanation: Assume $m = 2$, Column A is $x = \dfrac{22}{15}(2) = 2.93$ whereas column B is $y = \dfrac{43}{17}(2) = 5.058$. Therefore, column B is greater. The correct answer is (B).

48  **Answer: A**
Explanation: As it is known that 1 hour is equal to 60 minutes. Column A is,

    10 hours 35 minutes
    +2 hours 35 minutes
    12 hours 70 minutes

whereas column B is,

    8 hours 25 minutes
    −1 hours 15 minutes
    7 hours 10 minutes

Therefore, column A is greater. The correct answer is (A).

49  **Answer: A**
Explanation: Column A is $68.2 \times 10^3 = 682 \times 10^{-1} \times 10^3 = 68,200$ whereas column B is $6,820,000 \div 10^6 = \dfrac{682 \times 10^4}{10^6} = 6.82$. Therefore, column A is greater. The correct answer is (A).

50  **Answer: C**
Explanation: The absolute value of column A is $8|z - 3| = 8(z - 3)$ whereas column B is $8|3 - z| = 8|(-1)(z - 3)| = 8(z - 3)$. Therefore, both columns are equal. The correct answer is (C).

51  **Answer: A**
Explanation: Column A is $p(5) = 7(5)^6 = 109,375$ whereas column B is $p(9) = \dfrac{9(9) - 39}{9} = 4.666$. Therefore, column A is greater. The correct answer is (A).

**Grades 6 and above** | **Practice Test 3 Session 2**

---

**52** **Answer: B**

Explanation: Column A is $\dfrac{509/1045}{1078/524} = \dfrac{509 \cdot 524}{1078 \cdot 1045} = \dfrac{266{,}716}{1{,}126{,}510} = 0.2367$ whereas column B is $\dfrac{1{,}126{,}510}{266{,}716} = 4.2236$. Therefore, column B is greater. The correct answer is (B).

**53** **Answer: A**

Explanation: Column A is $0.978$ whereas column B is $0.879$. Therefore, column A is greater. The correct answer is (A).

**54** **Answer: B**

Explanation: Column A is $y = -\dfrac{20(-4)}{15} - 89 = -83.66$ whereas column B is $-4 = -\dfrac{2x}{15} + 43 \Rightarrow -47 = -\dfrac{2x}{15} \Rightarrow x = 352.5$. Therefore, column B is greater. The correct answer is (B).

**55** **Answer: C**

Explanation: Column A is $\dfrac{48}{14} \times \dfrac{54}{20} \times \dfrac{4}{9} = \dfrac{2592}{630} = 4.114$ whereas column B is $\dfrac{4}{20} \times \dfrac{48}{9} \times \dfrac{54}{20} = \dfrac{2592}{630} = 4.114$. Therefore, both columns are equal. The correct answer is (C).